Handy Household Hints

Published by
Nickel Press

Contents

Tips for Saving

**Let's face it, you work hard to earn your money,
so it only seems proper that we include ways to save
money in a book of labor–saving tips**

Shop Smart

Break the habit of buying the latest chemical cleaner,
food product or fancy gadget when a more basic solution
is available. It is amazing how much money we waste on
things just because they claim to be "new" or
"improved".

We don't want to start a debate with anyone attached to
a particular product, but for those who aren't... SHOP
AROUND. Dish and laundry detergents, for example, are
all pretty much the same. Our philosophy has always
been to try the least expensive product and then move up
if we don't like it for some reason. For laundry detergent
we buy the cheapest one that smells good!

——— ◆ ———

When shopping for an appliance, try to start with some
idea of what you want and the price you want to pay.
From hand mixers to refrigerators, today's products have
so many bells and whistles that one can easily spend a
lot of money for features that will never be used.

• Do you really need a twelve–speed blender? All we
  ever use is off and on.

HANDY HOUSEHOLD HINTS

- It certainly is wondrous to get ice water and ice cubes from a dispenser outside the refrigerator, but unless you have a large family that would otherwise be constantly opening and closing the refrigerator door, its not cost effective.
- Energy use can be an important consideration over the life of a major appliance, so take it into consideration—an energy–efficient unit that is a bit more expensive may be a sound investment.

---◆---

Save money on the larger size, sometimes. Generally, you can save money by buying the larger package, but not always. Compare the unit cost before you buy.

---◆---

When you compare prices, don't always trust the unit prices on the shelf labels; they are frequently wrong!

Okay, so you don't like to do the math. Then spend a couple of dollars for a hand–held calculator. When comparing the cost of two different items, enter the cost of one and divide by the number of units in the package (ounces, pieces, laundry loads, etc.). That will give you the unit price, but don't even look at it—just multiply it by the number of units in the second package. If you arrive at a number that is more than the cost of the second item, then it's the better buy. If your number is less, the first package is the better buy.

Don't mean to belabor this, but you will be amazed at how often the smaller package is a better buy... and easier to carry.

---◆---

Use coupons wisely. Coupons can save you money only if the reduced price is less than the brand you would normally buy. Coupons are generally associated with national brands that cost more than the store brand even with the reduction.

Keep in mind, too, that coupons are generally good for at least a couple of months. If you don't need the item right away, wait for it to go on sale for additional savings.

Our coupons are not terribly well–organized, but we do follow two rules: (1) always carry the coupons for things we buy often, just to see if we can get the item on sale; and (2) check for coupons that will expire in a couple of weeks to decide whether it's worthwhile to use them or to toss them out.

———— ◆ ————

Coupons can offer the opportunity to try a pricey product at a cost near that of the store brand. You may want to take advantage of coupons simply to find out if you prefer the premium brand which is, of course, what the coupons are intended to do. The next time you buy though, without a coupon, consider whether you prefer the product enough to pay a premium price for it.

———— ◆ ————

Sales can offer bargains, but only if the item is something you need and the sale price is truly a bargain. One store's sale may be another store's everyday price!

Sale items, called 'loss leaders', are intended to attract shoppers who will buy other products as well. If you are attracted to a new store by a sale, make sure that anything else you buy is in line with what you normally pay.

———— ◆ ————

A sale can be a good time to stock up. Buy extra packages of products you use regularly that keep well and anticipate needing within a reasonable period.

Store these 'backup' items in a special place so you don't forget that you have them the next time you make up a shopping list.

———◆———

Be diligent! If you focus on sale items, the system will eventually work and your larder will be well stocked.

———◆———

Grocery shopping when you are hungry often results in wasteful buying. The craving for food can lead you to buy expensive items whose only virtue is their ease of preparation, or to picking up an assortment of fresh produce and baked goods that have little chance of being consumed before they expire.

A little trick that may help if you haven't eaten is to drink part of your daily ration of water before you shop. Most markets have a water fountain; get in the habit of making it your first stop!

———◆———

Shopping without a list and buying on impulse can also be wasteful—you could wind up with a pantry full of exotic foods that you'll never use.

Planning the menu and making a list will also save the extra steps that you inevitably take if you work out your meal plan while you shop.

———◆———

Buy in bulk whenever it's economical, especially if it is something that you can portion out in reusable containers when you get home.

TIPS FOR SAVING

Avoid pre–packaged produce! Buy loose produce that you can inspect thoroughly.

———— ◆ ————

Place a hand basket in a shopping cart to hold loose fruits and vegetables instead of plastic bags from the produce department.
Use mesh bags you bring from home if you need to keep items separated.

———— ◆ ————

Those fancy packages cost money. When you purchase a product make sure you are paying for the product and not the packaging.
Those little juice packs complete with straws may be handy for a lunch box, but if they replace the large container in the refrigerator you are more than doubling the price of the juice you drink around the house.

———— ◆ ————

Prepared ingredients can be expensive as well.
Those of us not inclined to make a cake from scratch certainly appreciate the convenience (and quality) of bake mixes that require only adding eggs and water. We must be wary, however, not to fall into the convenience trap.
Packaged stuffing mixes, coatings for meat or vegetables, and flavored rice or pasta contain only herb and spice combinations that we normally have on our pantry shelf. They take only a few moments to prepare at home, cost a lot less, and we don't add a bunch of extra chemicals.

———— ◆ ————

Avoid expensive aerosol cans and their ozone–destroying vapors. Compare the cost—you'll find that you get much more product for the money in a spray bottle.

If you do have a pet product trapped in an aerosol can, dispose of the used container properly.

Most areas have collection points for hazardous products such as aerosol cans, used batteries, old paint, and other chemicals. Some even have collection days when they will pick up materials left at the curbside. Get in the habit of collecting these items in a sturdy trash bag and periodically dropping them off.

Save Energy, Save Money

Adding a little salt when heating water reduces the time it takes to come to a boil.

———— ◆ ————

Pot sizes for cooking should correspond to the burner size. Small pots on large burners waste heat and can cause scorched handles (and hands) as well.

———— ◆ ————

Covering a pot or kettle conserves energy, reduces warming or cooking time, and prevents loss to evaporation. Those wonderful kitchen odors represent a loss of flavor in the food you are cooking; a certain amount of aroma is great, too much can rob the food of its appeal. Particles from the evaporating water also add to those clinging to the walls that you will have to clean up later.

TIPS FOR SAVING

To save cooking time and energy cost, whenever practical, set refrigerated food out in sufficient time to allow it to reach room temperature before you are ready to start cooking.

◆

Save energy when heating water by heating only the amount you need, as for a cup of tea. You might want to set a timer to avoid boiling the small amount of liquid away if you leave the room.

◆

Reduce energy costs when using the oven by turning off the heat eight to ten minutes before cooking is complete. With the door closed, the food and the oven retain enough heat to finish the cooking.
Not a good idea for cakes or bread and the like that rely on constant heat for rising and to complete the baking.

◆

Avoid high heat when cooking with non-stick cookware. High heat wastes energy (and money), and is seldom necessary. In addition, it can shorten the life of the cookware by loosening the non-stick coating.

◆

Monitoring the thermostat can save energy. Comfort levels generally do not require extreme heat in winter or extreme cold in the summer.

◆

Turn air conditioning or heat down rather than off. In many cases, the energy consumption and strain on equipment to bring temperatures back to normal far outweigh any savings you might enjoy by turning them off.

Check air filters at least once a month and keep them clean. A clogged filter in a heating or air conditioning unit can restrict air flow, overwork the unit, and cost energy dollars, not to mention that you won't get the amount of heating or cooling that you expect.

———— ◆ ————

Curtains and drapes save energy because they create a pocket of air inside a window that acts as insulation.

———— ◆ ————

Seal off cracks around windows or doors where outside air creeps in to avoid further loss of heat or cooling.

———— ◆ ————

Washing dishes in a sink or pan of water uses far less water than washing and rinsing under running water.

———— ◆ ————

The dishwasher can save water and energy if you eliminate the dry cycle. Simply open the washer after the last rinse and allow the dishes to air dry.

———— ◆ ————

Mixer faucets can be an energy drain if the hot water heater is on. Most of the time you only want cold water and the mixer usually pulls at least some hot water.

———— ◆ ————

Set the hot water heater to a reasonable temperature. Higher temperatures cause the unit to heat and re–heat water that you never use.

You may want to try turning on the water heater only when you need it; most take only a few minutes to heat enough water for a shower or a load of dishes. At the very least, consider a timer that will turn the unit on and off at certain times of the day. The first month's saving on your utility bill will more than pay for the timer.

———— ◆ ————

Consider a water saver shower head. It uses less water, requires less hot water, and usually offers an improved spray in areas where water pressure is low.

———— ◆ ————

Save water by taking a shower. A normal shower uses one–third to one–half the water of a bath.

———— ◆ ————

To conserve water, place a brick in the toilet tank, making sure that it doesn't interfere with any moving parts. The brick will reduce the capacity of the tank and thus the amount of water used.
When placing the brick, flush the toilet and when the tank is emptied position it exactly where you want if.

———— ◆ ————

...or place a small plastic jug in the toilet tank. Water in the jug or container will hold it in place. You may have to experiment to determine the right size for your tank— one that saves water without interfering with proper flushing.

———— ◆ ————

Use lower wattage bulbs wherever they offer enough light. It would be counterproductive to skimp on lighting over a work area or reading chair, but most areas don't require a lot of light. Some may even benefit from the soft, soothing light of a bulb that isn't too bright.

Low wattage or appliance bulbs are usually best for closed fixtures. The heat generated by the bulb within the fixture can't escape and it tends to shorten bulb life, so the lower wattage that creates less heat usually offers longer life.

Appliance bulbs used in ovens and refrigerators tend to be more expensive than regular bulbs and are designed to better withstand extremes in temperature. We have noticed, however, that in some fixtures the appliance bulb does no better than a regular one.

We checked by marking the package with the date the bulb was installed and when it failed, replaced it with a regular one and marked its package. When the regular bulb failed, we were able to decide which to use in the future based on the time each bulb lasted and their relative cost.

◆

So–called energy saver bulbs are not necessarily a bargain. They usually cost more than regular bulbs, and studies have shown that they provide less light. Generally it is most economical to buy the less expensive bulb at the wattage you need.

◆

Fix that leak! You would be amazed at the amount of water (and money) lost through a leaky faucet or toilet tank. Not to mention that the constant dripping of water can destroy the fixture. And if the overflow valve of a hot water tank is faulty, you can waste electricity or gas as well.

◆

Fluorescent tubes last longer if they are not turned off and on too often; use them in areas that are usually lit for long periods.

Make the Best Use of Everything

Save those plastic bags from the store—depending on their size, they can be used for storage, lining small trash cans, covering hands when working with messy wood stains or harsh cleaners, etc.

———— ◆ ————

Make a handy plastic bag holder:
Cut the sleeve from an old shirt that you plan to recycle. Sew one end (or staple it, if you aren't concerned about being fancy), leaving a small opening. Stuff bags in the other end and close the top with a piece of string, a rubber band, or a twist tie. You can then pull a bag out through the small hole whenever you need one.
Hang the holder on the door of a cupboard near the trash, in a cleaning closet, or wherever you are most likely to use the bags.

———— ◆ ————

...and a cleaning rag holder:
Make a sleeve holder as described above for cleaning rags as well. Or make several: one for the kitchen, one for the bath, one to carry around in the cleaner bucket or caddy, and one for the workshop, garage, or anywhere else rags are often needed.

———— ◆ ————

Used containers that held deodorant or cologne can be placed on a closet shelf or in a drawer to give off a pleasant fragrance for a long time.

11

Occasionally you may have to buy something in an over-priced fancy package. Get a return on your investment if you can—some make attractive storage containers for things often left out on the counter such as for pasta, sugar, candy, crackers, etc.

◆

Get a little more use from a dried–out felt marker by soaking for ten or fifteen minutes in a cup of water to which a tablespoon of vinegar has been added. Gently massage the tip to leech out the vinegar, replace the top and allow to rest for a day. The color may be a bit light at first, but it will improve with use.

This works for a usable marker left out with the cap removed. Sorry, but it won't help an old marker that has simply run out of ink.

◆

Freeze nail polish to make it last longer.

◆

Freeze panty hose to make them more durable.

◆

Protect valuable televisions, stereos and computers with surge protectors. Good quality single plug connectors are not terribly expensive and while nothing can handle a direct hit by lightning, they do protect against damage from most power surges.

Anyone who has a considerable investment in electronic equipment should consider investing a bit more in a surge protector that includes insurance against anything, including a direct hit by lightning—if the equipment doesn't survive, it is replaced.

Don't overprotect—it can be expensive! Have you noticed how everyone wants to sell extended coverage on everything you buy? Think about it before you accept.

We were recently offered two year extended coverage for repairs on a new appliance that would have increased the cost by twenty percent. But the manufacturer already warrantees it for one year, and our experience with quality appliances has been that if they don't have a manufacturing defect that shows up in the first few months, they will last for years. It's your call, but think about it!

———— ◆ ————

Consider all of your insurance in the same light. If you can afford to cover the cost of minor damage to your car or home, opt for a larger deductible and pocket the extra premium you save. Think of insurance as protection against catastrophic loss such as the total destruction of your car or home and their contents.

Keep in mind that insurance companies make a profit or they wouldn't be in business, which means that the odds of not having to pay out for a claim are in their favor. It is therefore in your best interest to accept as much of the risk as you comfortably can.

All Around the Kitchen

The kitchen is more than a place to prepare food; it is the heart of the home that often serves as a gathering place. The kitchen needs to be maintained as a space that is pleasant for its occupants, especially the cook.

Keep your kitchen clean and sparkling. Wipe down spigots and sinks after using them.

Create a pleasant aroma by simmering a small pot of water with a couple of sticks of cinnamon in it on a back burner.

A refrigerator containing ready snacks such as carrot sticks, cleaned celery, or cheese cubes is always inviting.

Keep the cookie jar filled with healthy snacks as well.

ALL AROUND THE KITCHEN

Add a floral arrangement or live plants on a window sill to brighten up the kitchen.

If the kitchen does not have a window, hang a framed mirror without a border on an unused wall and hang light kitchen curtains over and around the sides.

Shopping

Buying the best quality means better nutrition, less waste, and less chance of contracting a food–borne illness

When buying chicken look for clear skin and light yellow fat. Brown patches on the skin are evidence of freezer burn caused by thawing and re–freezing—usually the result of poor handling.

Avoid stuffed frozen fowl as there is a risk of contamination if the bird is allowed to defrost improperly before cooking. In addition, the cost per pound may be more than for a plain whole bird and at the very least, you're paying meat prices for bread stuffing.

Marinade on meats can camouflage poor quality. They too, are often more expensive than plain meat and the liquid adds weight so that you wind up buying some very expensive water with the meat.

Whole fish in the market should have bulging eyes, shiny scales, firm flesh, and no unpleasant odor. Fish fillets should exhibit moist firm flesh and an absence of any unpleasant odor.

In short, fish should not smell of ammonia or "fishy"—if it does, don't buy it.

When buying fruit, look for clean, unbruised skin.

To hasten ripening at home, place the fruit in a brown bag and store at room temperature, but check daily to be sure it doesn't get overripe.

Sometimes tomatoes will ripen on a sunny windowsill. Place them on a plate, green side up, and check often to be sure they don't start to rot.

Select heads of lettuce that are tight and firm. Check for rust—even a few dark spots can indicate a head that is much worse inside.

Fresh beans and peas should be crisp and bright green.

Zucchini and yellow squash should have bright, clear, shiny skin.

Melon should have a fragrant aroma and you should be able to depress the ends slightly when you hold one in your hands and press firmly with the thumbs.

A ripe watermelon will give off a hollow sound when you thump it.

A ripe pineapple will release its leaves with a gentle pull and emit a sweet, rich aroma.

Shake a coconut to hear the 'milk' sloshing inside. Without that sound, the coconut is probably not fresh or has been cracked, good reasons not to buy it.

Check potatoes and onions by smelling for rot and pressing them to see that they are firm.
Recheck bagged produce when you get home from the market. One overlooked rotting potato or onion can spoil the entire batch in short order.

The best frozen vegetables are those that are loose in the package. Chunks of vegetables frozen solid are an indication that the package has been allowed to thaw and re–freeze. Be wary, too, of frozen food packages covered with ice crystals.

Check the dates on milk and other dairy products. These are 'sell by' dates—the product is expected to remain fresh for at least a few days after the date, but why not buy the freshest food you can get?

Keeping Food Fresh

Rewrap meat, poultry, or fish for refrigerating or freezing as soon as you get it home from the market. Throw away the pad customarily placed under poultry or meat to soak up moisture to keep the package dry in the store.

———— ◆ ————

Fat hastens spoilage, so if you don't want it on the meat, cut it off before you repackage. This is a fine opportunity to portion the meat as well—if you plan to use only half a chicken for a meal or the breasts for one meal and thighs for another, cut them up right away so that you need only defrost the amount you want for a meal.

Poultry does not keep well in the refrigerator. It should be used within a few days, whether raw or cooked. Chicken keeps better than turkey or duck, and a whole fowl can be kept longer than parts.

Ground meat spoils quicker than solid meat and should not be stored in the refrigerator for more than a couple of days. That's because the ground meat has more surface area exposed to the air where bacteria can thrive.
If not to be used quickly, the meat should be frozen as soon as it is brought home from the market.

Fish should be used soon after buying—don't store in the refrigerator for more than a day or two.

Fish stored in the refrigerator should be iced with proper drainage so that the flesh does not soak up water.
The ice needs to be directly on the fish—remove fish from the store wrapping, rinse it well, and place it in a plastic bag. Place the bag in a colander or sieve over a catch bowl and cover with ice. Then cover the whole thing in plastic wrap to avoid adding aroma to other things in the refrigerator.

The best way to defrost meat if time allows, is in the refrigerator tightly wrapped.

Meat can be defrosted quickest in a water–tight wrap in cold water. Don't defrost in the air or use hot water as both hasten the growth of bacteria.

Soften brown sugar by putting a slice of soft bread in the package. Close the package and the sugar will loosen up in a couple of hours.

Frozen bread defrosts in a few minutes at room temperature. For a fresh bread smell and texture, place the loaf in a brown paper bag and bake at 250° for about three minutes.

To prevent salt from caking, put a small amount of uncooked rice in the salt shaker. The rice lasts for a long time in all but the most humid of climates, but it does need to be changed occasionally.

Freeze bananas when they turn black! Just toss them in a plastic bag in the freezer, then peel with a knife and use for baking in bread and cake, or make smoothies by blending with milk and a little ice.

Store garlic cloves, peeled, in a small jar of olive or other oil. After a time, the oil itself can be used to add a light taste of garlic to a salad dressing or cooked dish.

ALL AROUND THE KITCHEN

Iced tea will keep longer if sugar is not added until just before the tea is served. If the tea is cold, mix the desired amount of sugar with just enough hot water to dissolve it before mixing it with the tea.

Food will keep longer in the refrigerator or freezer if it is placed in a tightly closed plastic bag or container that contains a minimum of excess air.

Store coffee in the freezer to keep it fresh. The flavor of coffee comes from an essential oil that can dry out at room temperature.

Cut the tops off root vegetables before storing; tops left on will siphon nutrients and flavor from the vegetable.

Line the refrigerator crispers with paper toweling to keep vegetables fresh longer and make cleanup a snap—just fold up the toweling to trap particles and discard.

Store potatoes in a cool place, but do not refrigerate them which will turn the starch to sugar.

Potatoes will spoil more quickly if stored near onions.

HANDY HOUSEHOLD HINTS

Freeze fresh fruits and vegetables by spreading slices of fresh, ripe squash, zucchini, green peppers, berries, etc. on a cookie sheet and placing them in the freezer overnight. Once frozen, they can be packaged in a manner most convenient for your use, that is, in meal-sized or portion–sized units.

Vegetables need to be blanched before freezing if they are to retain their color.

Leftover fat from deep fat frying will keep best in the refrigerator if residual food particles are first removed by straining the fat through several layers of cheesecloth or toweling placed in a strainer.

Cottage cheese, yogurt, sour cream, etc. fare better in the refrigerator when stored upside down to keep out air and the microorganisms that promote spoilage.

Never eat from a container that is to be returned to the refrigerator. Saliva can introduce enzymes that will begin to break down the food even if it is properly stored.

Store foods in the refrigerator and pantry so that the oldest is used first; when unpacking groceries, put the newest items in the back.

Keep bagged food fresh by folding the top down two or three times and holding it tight with a clothespin or paper clip after opening.

ALL AROUND THE KITCHEN

Place paper or cardboard dry food containers in plastic containers or zip lock bags as soon as they come from the grocer's. It will help maintain freshness while keeping out bugs and rodents.

Store leftovers in the refrigerator in:
- clear containers that allow you to see what's in them without taking everything out of the refrigerator;
- square or rectangular containers that take up less room; and
- stackable containers to save even more room.

To keep seeds and nuts fresh, freeze them. Freezing preserves the oils that are the essence of their flavor.
This also applies to flour, cereal and chips.

Crackers stay fresh in the freezer if you are careful to wrap them securely to keep out moisture.

To save part of an onion, rub the cut side with butter, wrap in plastic wrap and refrigerate.

Uncooked peeled potatoes can be stored in the refrigerator for three or four days if they are kept in water with a few drops of vinegar in it.

Unpopped popcorn will stay fresh longer in the freezer and there will be fewer unpopped kernels. Outside air robs the corn of the moisture it needs to pop well.

To keep ice cream fresh, top with a piece of plastic wrap or waxed paper pressed down over the unused portion in the container.

Toss out moldy bread without opening the package. Mold spores can live a long time in the air—an opened package may contaminate the kitchen and hasten spoilage of the next loaf.
If you have a persistent problem with moldy bread, sponge out the bread box with vinegar water and allow it to air dry thoroughly.

Surfaces that have been in contact with mold should be wiped down thoroughly with vinegar and water.

Preparation

Defrost chicken before cooking. Chicken cooked from the frozen state produces a red, "bloody" juice rather than clear liquid after it is cooked and never looks done near the bone.

Chicken or turkey should be rinsed thoroughly before cooking to rid it of any contamination.

To tell when chicken or pork is done, pierce the meat about halfway through at the thickest part with a small knife; if the liquid runs clear, the meat is done.

Refresh your fish! Before preparing previously frozen seafood or shellfish, soak it for a few minutes in salted water—it will smell fresh from the sea.

Thaw fish or shellfish in milk to restore fresh flavor.

It's not necessary to overcook pork. Cook until the internal temperature is 140° or until there is no redness in the meat and the juices run clear.

To properly brown meat, dry thoroughly with paper towels, be sure the oil in the pan is very hot but not smoking, and don't crowd the pan. If these steps are followed, the meat will brown quickly without sticking to the pan.
Crowding the meat traps heat and causes it to steam. In the presence of steam, it will cook without browning, giving up flavorful juices in the process.

To make carving easier, allow a large piece of meat or poultry to rest for fifteen to twenty minutes after cooking. This will congeal or 'set' the juices and provide a firmer texture for cutting.

Casseroles need to rest after cooking to firm up. Let dishes such as lasagna or macaroni and cheese sit for ten to fifteen minutes after you take them out of the oven.

Pop the core out of a head of lettuce by striking the head on a countertop, core side down. The core will break loose and you can easily pull it out.

ALL AROUND THE KITCHEN

To keep from crying while cutting onions cut the top end first, then rinse hands, knife, cutting board and the onion with cold water. Periodically rinse your hands and the knife while chopping.

Avoid tears by peeling onions under cold running water.

Place onions in the refrigerator or freezer for a few minutes before cutting to slow down the action of the chemical that irritates the eyes.

When peeling onions, hold a wooden match in your teeth—the sulfur will attract the chemical that makes your eyes burn.

Onions make you cry because they irritate your sinuses, so try breathing through you mouth while slicing. It really works!

To fry without sticking, heat the pan before adding oil or butter.

When frying with butter over high heat, use half butter and half cooking oil to keep the butter from smoking or browning. The cooking oil has a higher smoking point and will protect the butter.

When fat reaches the smoking point, that is, it literally begins to smoke, discard it and start over.
Whether for pan frying or deep frying, once the fat starts to break down, it loses flavor and the ability to stay hot enough to cook properly.

To prevent spattering grease, sprinkle a little salt in a frying pan.

To tenderize meat while boiling, add a tablespoon of vinegar to the water.

Beef can be tenderized with water! Allow thinly cut slices of beef to soak in water for a few hours or overnight to break down the fibers.

To tenderize and flavor beef or game let it soak in a marinade of wine or in a mixture of three parts bouillon and one part vinegar. Vary the portions of bouillon and vinegar to suit your taste.

For a different flavor, marinate beef or game in your favorite salad dressing. A vinegar based dressing will tenderize as well; creamy dressings add flavor with less tenderizing.

For outstanding baked or barbecued chicken soak in bouillon, salad dressing thinned with water, wine, or beer for an hour or two prior to cooking. We found a commercial Italian dressing that isn't to our taste on salad, but makes a great marinade for barbecued chicken.

To season chicken well, create a pocket between the skin and the meat and rub the seasoning there. Once started, the skin can be easily pulled away from the meat.
This is particularly effective for those who cook chicken with the skin on to keep it moist and then serve it without the skin to reduce calories and fat.

Prevent fresh cut fruit from browning by tossing with a little lemon juice. The juice from half a lemon is sufficient for a quart of cut fruit.

To sweeten cut fruit and keep it from browning, cover it with simple syrup.
Make simple syrup by boiling equal parts of sugar and water until the sugar is dissolved.

When measuring syrup or honey rub a little cooking oil in the measuring cup or spoon before you use it to keep the liquid from sticking to the spoon and rinse in hot water when you are done. If a recipe calls for butter or oil, measure that first, then use the coated spoon for measuring the sticky stuff.

To lightly thicken sauces or soups, blend two tablespoons of butter and two tablespoons of flour with a fork and shape it into small balls. Drop them, one at a time, into the hot liquid, stirring as the sauce thickens. Do not let the liquid boil—merely cook sufficiently to dispel the raw flour taste.
This is similar to a mixture the French call *Buerre Manié*, used to bind certain sauces. The two tablespoon mixture is enough to thicken one cup of liquid.

To get gelatin out of the mold easily, before filling, rinse the mold in cold water and dry it, then coat the inside with salad oil. The oil will leave a nice glaze on the gelatin.

Make perfect hard–boiled eggs by placing the eggs in a pan of cold water, bringing the water to a boil and then letting the pan sit off the heat, covered, for fifteen minutes.
The eggs will cook gently which keeps the white from getting rubbery.

To keep boiled eggs from cracking when they cook, pierce the bottom of the eggs with a pin before placing them in the pan. Piercing them in this way also allows gas trapped in the base to escape, allowing the egg to fill out the shell and improve the shape if the eggs are to be served whole.

For easy peeling of hard–boiled eggs, drain off the cooking water, shake the eggs in the pan to crack the shells, then place them in a bowl of water with ice in it. After a couple of minutes, the shells will come off easily. If the first one doesn't peel easily, allow them to remain in the ice water a little longer.

To determine if an egg is hard–boiled or raw, set the egg up on the small end and spin it like a top. Really! The hard–boiled egg will spin; the raw egg will fall over.

To beat fluffy egg whites, there must be no trace of yolk in the whites, the whites should be at room temperature,

31

and the utensils must be absolutely clean.
The white will not expand properly if there is the tiniest bit of grease left on the bowl, on the whisk, or from the yolks. To avoid getting yolk into the whites, separate eggs one at a time over a small bowl, then add them to the mixing bowl. That way, if a yolk breaks, you have only one egg that you have to set aside for scrambling later instead of the whole lot.

For fluffier scrambled eggs or omelets, the eggs should be at room temperature before beating.

Make a fluffy omelet by adding a little water and beating well.

For a richer omelet, add a little milk or cream.

To get the catsup started, insert a knife or soda straw a few inches into the bottle to break the air lock.

To keep sliced bananas from darkening, toss them with a little lemon juice.

ALL AROUND THE KITCHEN

Wash fresh vegetables in cold water. Hot water leeches out vitamins and minerals.

When cutting vegetables or kneading dough on a cutting board, cover the countertop under the board with newspaper. It will absorb moisture, collect stray vegetable clippings or flour, and generally make cleanup a lot easier.

When warming food in the microwave, cover it with a wicker paper plate holder. The wicker will prevent spatters while allowing steam to escape; and it can be easily cleaned by rinsing with hot water afterward.

When warming rolls in the microwave, place them on a ridged rack or crumpled aluminum foil, or elevate them with toothpicks to keep the bottoms from getting soggy.

To make coffee less acidic, top the grounds with a teaspoon or two of sugar before you brew. Even those who take coffee without sugar shouldn't find it too sweet, just pleasant tasting.

For international coffee without an international price, add flavoring when you brew. Top the ground coffee

33

with a little vanilla, cinnamon, rum flavoring, almond extract, chocolate, or a combination to suit your taste.

Be careful about substituting commercial bouillon or reconstituted cubes in recipes that call for meat or vegetable stock. Bouillon is largely salt, so even cutting back or eliminating salt called for in the recipe may not be satisfactory.

We're inclined to mix the bouillon at half strength, eliminate any additional salt and see if the rest of the ingredients will carry the day. Then, if they don't, we correct the seasoning with additional bouillon at the end of the cooking.

There are quality substitutes, called meat or vegetable *extract* that are not nearly as salty, but we use them with the same caution as with bouillon.

A combination of fresh vegetables will often turn the water in which they are cooked into a flavorful broth; if a recipe containing vegetables such as onions and carrots calls for bouillon, you may want to add it after cooking to see if you really need it.

Leaving out the bouillon may require adding salt, herbs, or otherwise adjusting the seasoning.

Bouillon can add flavor to broth; if your soup or stew turns out a little flat because the ingredients lacked character, a little bouillon may help.

Be creative with leftovers. Think of them as ingredients for a new dish—make them into soup; add a different sauce; or add other ingredients to make a new dish.

However, if the dish became a leftover because it was improperly prepared or no one liked it, bite the bullet and toss it.

Think ahead about leftovers. If you are making a dish that can serve for more than one meal, consider how you can alter it for the second meal. A vegetable, pasta, or rice dish can serve as a side dish for one meal and with the addition of meat or cheese as a main dish for another.

A white sauce lightly spiced can be changed dramatically by adding tomatoes or tomato sauce and Italian seasoning; or curry powder with raisins and coconut; or chili powder with peppers and onions.

It's not necessary to pre-cook the pasta before baking lasagna. Add a few tablespoons of water around the edges if the sauce is very thick, but take care not to add too much, and bake the dish covered.

Test with a fork after normal cooking time to be sure that the pasta is done. If not, cook a little longer, adding more water if necessary.

Try this technique once or twice and you will get the hang of if. The reward is a better tasting dish with one less step in its preparation.

Lasagna freezes well when prepared as described above. It can also be frozen *before* cooking. Simply defrost in the refrigerator and allow a little more cooking time.

Experiment with herbs and spices for a change of pace. A little nutmeg in spaghetti sauce, a bit of allspice in a chicken dish, cinnamon in sweet potatoes and carrots, nutmeg in spinach, or basil with almost any vegetable can create a touch of elegance.

The trick to experimenting with unfamiliar herbs and spices is to start with a little, then add more of what pleases you if necessary. Next try combinations in the same manner.

Do some creative mixing: blend carrots in the whipped potatoes, toss peas or raisins in spaghetti sauce, add mushroom slices to peas, or chop scallions in a white sauce to top another vegetable.

Save the leftover juice from pickles to marinate raw vegetables for garnish or snacks. The marinade will keep them fresh longer, too.

A bit of juice from pickles makes a tasty addition to cooked vegetables and salad dressings.

ALL AROUND THE KITCHEN

To prevent pots from boiling over, add a teaspoon of oil or butter to the water and don't close the lid tight.
Works for oatmeal, pasta, rice, split pea soup, and other starchy foods.

When you need softened butter for a recipe, grate a stick of butter—it will soften quickly.

Be careful using the microwave to soften butter—use low heat in five second intervals to be sure that the butter doesn't melt. *Melted butter* reacts differently in recipes than *soft butter*.

To shell walnuts and get whole pieces every time, soak the nuts overnight in salted water, then crack gently.

Use leftover baked potatoes to make potato salad.

Leftover baked potato can be diced and fried for speedy hash browns or cottage fries.

Use leftover mashed or baked potato to make a casserole: Line the bottom of the dish with a ground meat and vegetable mixture, fill with mashed or sliced potatoes, and top with cheese; bake at 350° for about 25 minutes or until cheese is bubbly.

To make opening fresh oysters or clams easier, leave them in the freezer for about an hour before opening.

Save time and energy by cooking two meals at once. When you make a popular dish that keeps well in the refrigerator or freezer, double the recipe to make a second meal for serving at a later time.

Save vegetable trimmings for the stock pot. Those trimmings may look nasty, but they are packed with flavor. Most of the wilted and tough parts of celery, carrots, onions, etc. can be cooked in water to make soup stock. If clarified, the stock will keep in the freezer for months.

To keep tea from being bitter, don't squeeze the moisture out of the leaves or bag back into the pitcher.

Substitutions

One teaspoon of arrowroot, as a thickener in a recipe, can be replaced by two teaspoons of flour or one and one–half teaspoons of cornstarch.

———— ◆ ————

One cup of buttermilk can be replaced by one cup of yogurt or one cup of sweet milk with two tablespoons of vinegar.

———— ◆ ————

One ounce of unsweetened chocolate can be replaced with three tablespoons of cocoa and one tablespoon of butter or margarine.

———— ◆ ————

Five ounces of semisweet chocolate can be replaced by three ounces of unsweetened chocolate and four tablespoons of sugar.

———— ◆ ————

Five ounces of semisweet chocolate can be replaced by one–quarter cup plus one tablespoon of cocoa, three tablespoons of butter or margarine and four tablespoons of sugar

———— ◆ ————

Coconut milk or coconut cream may be replaced in a recipe with the same quantity of regular milk or cream, but of course you lose the coconut flavor.

A cup of cracker crumbs can be replaced with one and one-third cups of bread crumbs.

———— ◆ ————

One cup of whipping cream can be replaced in some recipes with five ounces of butter and six ounces of milk.

———— ◆ ————

One cup of sour cream can be replaced by three tablespoons of butter and six ounces of yogurt.

———— ◆ ————

One cup of sifted cake flour can be replaced by one cup less two tablespoons of sifted all-purpose flour.

———— ◆ ————

One tablespoon of flour for thickening can be replaced by one and one-half tablespoons of cornstarch. Don't forget that cornstarch must be mixed well in cold water before being added to hot liquid.

———— ◆ ————

One cup of honey can be replaced by one cup of sugar plus one-quarter cup of liquid.

———— ◆ ————

One teaspoon of lemon juice can be replaced by one-half teaspoon of vinegar in some recipes.

———— ◆ ————

Maple sugar can be replaced in a recipe by an equal quantity of granulated sugar. Use maple extract to correct the flavor.

Maple sugar can be replaced by twice the quantity of maple syrup and adjusting the liquid in the recipe.

———— ◆ ————

One teaspoon of dry mustard can be replaced by one tablespoon of prepared mustard.

———— ◆ ————

Brown sugar may be replaced with an equal quantity of granulated sugar for small difference in taste and texture.

———— ◆ ————

Jelly or marmalade makes a delightful fruit syrup. Simply heat on the stove or in a microwave to melt. Serve over biscuits, pancakes, etc.

Correcting Problems

To correct salty soup or stew add a raw potato and allow it to cook for a bit. The potato will absorb the salt and can then be discarded.

———— ◆ ————

A broth that is too salty may be improved with the addition of sugar and vinegar. Try one teaspoonful of sugar and, if necessary, add one–half to one teaspoonful of vinegar to correct the flavor.

A sauce or vegetable that is too sweet can be corrected with salt or vinegar. Just a little will do it.

———— ◆ ————

To revive wilted vegetables remove the brown edges, rinse in cold water and refrigerate on a bed of damp paper towels in a plastic container with a tight fitting lid.

———— ◆ ————

Wilted vegetables may be revived by soaking in ice water in the refrigerator for an hour.

———— ◆ ————

To make old potato chips crisp, place them under the broiler briefly, taking care not to brown them.

———— ◆ ————

Use old potato or corn chips to top potatoes au gratin or tuna casserole.

———— ◆ ————

Old corn chips can be crumbled and transformed into Taco Pie when you top them with chili and cheese. Just heat in the microwave for about a minute and... ole!

———— ◆ ————

To make cereal and crackers crisp, place them on a cookie sheet and heat them for a few minutes in the oven.

———— ◆ ————

A better use for old crackers is to make crumbs to coat fried fish, chicken, or pork chops.

To smooth lumpy gravy or sauce, force it through a strainer, then whisk constantly while reheating.

———— ◆ ————

Very sour fruit can be improved with the addition of a small amount of salt. It will then require less sugar to sweeten.

———— ◆ ————

Sticky rice can sometimes be improved by rinsing with warm water.

———— ◆ ————

To refresh bread or rolls, sprinkle them with a few drops of water, place them in a paper bag, and heat in a 250° to 300° oven for a few minutes.

———— ◆ ————

To remove excess fat from broth, soup or gravy, refrigerate the liquid until the fat hardens on top and can be lifted off.

———— ◆ ————

For quick fat removal, add ice cubes to the broth. The grease will cling to the ice cubes for easy removal.

———— ◆ ————

Honey that has crystallized can be restored by heating. Pour the honey into a small saucepan, preferably non-stick, or place the jar on a trivet in water in the saucepan, and heat slowly. Do not heat with the jar in direct contact with the bottom of the pan as it may crack.

43

Kitchen Tools

Kitchen shears save a lot of hassles. Use them to open cellophane packages, snip parsley and green onions, trim crust from bread, cut up dried fruit and marshmallows, clip those coupons, etc.

——————— ◆ ———————

Keep a screwdriver in the kitchen for tightening screws on appliances, drawer pulls, etc. as soon as they become loose to avert a possible disaster later.

——————— ◆ ———————

Use a peg board to hang cookware and kitchen tools. They will be at hand when you need them and may add an interesting decorator touch.
Some kitchen cabinets have a small lip underneath next to the kitchen wall that provides sufficient space for a nail or hook—use them to hang pans or utensils in a place where you are most likely to need them.

——————— ◆ ———————

When you don't have the right size funnel, make one from several layers of aluminum foil or butcher paper rolled into a cone shape. Snip off the end to get the exact size opening you need.

——————— ◆ ———————

Make a pastry tube for piping soft fillings such as deviled egg from a heavy duty plastic storage bag. Cut off a corner of the bag for an opening the size you need for the job you are doing.

Storage

Avoid scratching good china by placing paper plates between the china plates before stacking.

———— ◆ ————

Store the good china in zip–lock bags. It prevents scratching and assures that it will be clean when you want to use it.

———— ◆ ————

Organizing pantry and refrigerator storage makes finding things easier. Keep like items together in the pantry and in the refrigerator.

———— ◆ ————

Use trays to keep small items together such as soup mixes, spices or seasonings in the pantry and condiments or cheeses in the refrigerator.

Working in the Kitchen

For cutting "sticky" foods, such as dried fruit, first dip the knife or shears in water, flour or powdered sugar.

———— ◆ ————

Grow your own herbs in pots or a planter in the kitchen. In addition to convenience for cooking, they add a wonderful decorator touch.

———— ◆ ————

To store herbs, lay them out on a paper towel in the refrigerator to dry for two or three days, then store in air–tight containers. Be sure that the herbs are really dry before storing or they may grow moldy.

———— ◆ ————

When pouring hot liquid into a glass container put a metal spoon, preferably silver, into the container and slowly pour the liquid onto the spoon. The metal will attract and disperse the heat.

———— ◆ ————

Try using a piece of sandpaper to get a grip on a stubborn jar lid.

———— ◆ ————

Inverting a jar in hot water for a few minutes may help to loosen the lid.

ALL AROUND THE KITCHEN

Jar lids held tight by dried food on the rim, may be loosened by gently lifting the lid with the edge of a spoon.

———— ◆ ————

A stubborn jar lid may be held tighter because of the vacuum inside the container. Piercing the lid with an ice pick or a nail will release the pressure and make the lid easier to remove.

———— ◆ ————

Remove a stuck bottle cap or cork by grasping with a nutcracker and twisting gently.

———— ◆ ————

Keep roaches out of the dishwasher by adding a couple of tablespoons of bleach when you wash dishes.

———— ◆ ————

Season a wooden cutting board by rubbing in boiled linseed oil and leaving to dry overnight.

———— ◆ ————

Poultry can leave harmful bacteria on the cutting board or counter top. Clean the surface, utensils, and hands thoroughly with soapy water immediately after preparing chicken, turkey, etc. Dish washing detergent is a great disinfectant.

Periodically disinfect cutting boards with a solution of one part bleach to ten parts water. Rinse with a vinegar and water solution.

47

The can opener is one of the worst germ carriers in the kitchen. Wash it with soap and water after every use. Scrub it thoroughly from time to time with a brush to eliminate the buildup of food on the blade and gears.

———— ◆ ————

Stuff snacks with a pastry tube. Soft mixtures for filling deviled eggs, stuffing celery, or topping crackers can be piped through a pastry tube quickly with less mess, and, if a decorator tip is used, with professional looking results.

———— ◆ ————

Recycle old bath towels. Cut them up for use as utility towels when working in the kitchen. Saves on paper towels.

———— ◆ ————

Place an old towel in the bottom of the sink when washing dishes as a cushion against breakage

———— ◆ ————

To find a stray knife in the dish water, use a tall glass like a telescope to see through the suds to the bottom of the pan.

———— ◆ ————

When you have only a partial load for the dish washer, fill it out with seldom–used dishes or glassware. That way they will always be clean when you need them.

Hang a decorative print, framed, with a glass cover on the wall behind the sink. When you wash dishes, drape an old towel over the print to catch splashes. Then use the towel to wipe down the sink and counters.

———◆———

Prevent messy drips from oil or syrup containers by wrapping the neck with a paper towel or a piece of cloth folded down to about a two inch band and securing it with a rubber band. The collar will catch the drips before they make a mess.

———◆———

Place a carpet remnant on the floor where you often work, as in front of the sink or counter; it will reduce fatigue and catch any spills.

———◆———

If you tend to leave kitchen drawers open when you work, they are bound to catch some crumbs and other debris now and then. Use a vacuum cleaner hose fitted with a crevice tool to clean them out quickly.

———◆———

And don't forget the toaster—most have a removable tray in the bottom that catches the crumbs. Clean it out regularly to avoid attracting vermin.

———◆———

Cover the bottom of the oven with heavy foil to catch spills and make cleanup easier.

Use only plastic or wood utensils on non–stick cookware—metal scratches, and eventually the non–stick surface is transferred to food.
There's no benefit to having scratches on the bottom of *any* cookware, so we recommend plastic or wood whenever practical.

———— ◆ ————

To find out if a dish is suitable for use in the microwave: Place a cup of cold water and the empty dish in the microwave; run on high for one minute. If the water is warm and the empty dish is cold it is fine for cooking in the microwave; if the dish is warm it can be used for short periods, as in re–heating or defrosting; if it is hot, keep it out of the microwave—you want the food to absorb the heat, not the dish.

———— ◆ ————

To cure an iron pan, cover it with a thin coat of oil and bake in a 250° oven for about two hours. Turn off the oven and allow the pan to cool in the oven.
If you don't mind the aroma, a pan can be cured over low heat on top of the stove as well. But be careful that it doesn't overheat.

———— ◆ ————

An iron pan may be cured or have its cure revived by using it for deep frying.

———— ◆ ————

To maintain the cure on an iron pan, wipe clean after each use with a dry paper towel. If necessary, use hot water and a plastic or nylon scrubber. After cleaning, cover the cooking surface with a light coat of oil. If treated properly, the cure will improve with each use.

Entertaining

**If you enjoy spontaneous gatherings,
keep a list of quick meals and snacks
to jog your memory.**

———— ◆ ————

Keep a supply of ingredients for quick dishes that can be prepared quickly and easily stretched if the number of guests grows. Good bets to have on hand are:

• Canned nuts and dried fruit for quick snacks, garnish for an entrée, or dessert
• Canned tuna, sardines, smoked oysters or mussels for appetizers or to garnish a salad or entrée
• Olives or pickles for garnish
• Frozen breadstuffs such as pita or tortillas
• Canned vegetables, especially an assortment of legumes such as pinto beans, navy beans, or garbanzos that can be quickly turned into soup or a main dish.
• Canned Italian–style tomato sauce (or a frozen container of your own special sauce)
• A variety of pasta
• A good selection of herbs and spices such as basil, thyme, sage, bay leaf, oregano, curry, and chili powder.

Over time you will probably accumulate more, but this is a good basic group for starters.

The above selections, coupled with any fresh items you normally have on hand such as fruit, vegetables, cheese, etc. can provide the means to prepare a wide variety of quick meals for a crowd.

Quick Appetizer Idea #1: Antipasto—Cut up fresh vegetables, cheese and cold cuts on a platter lined with lettuce; dribble oil and vinegar over and sprinkle with Parmesan cheese. Vary the ingredients to suit your taste or what you have available.
Serves equally well as buffet finger (or toothpick) food or at a sit–down dinner, with the platter as the centerpiece.

———— ◆ ————

Quick Appetizer Idea #2: Quick soup—Heat about ½ cup of water per person; flavor with bouillon; add minced celery, onions, scallions, tomato, etc., whatever you have, and boil for about five minutes; add leftover cooked vegetables or meat from the refrigerator to taste; heat and serve.

———— ◆ ————

Quick Appetizer Idea #3: Quick creamed soup—Same as quick soup with half the water; at the end mix in milk, cream or sour cream; heat, but do not allow to boil; garnish with a sprig of parsley, slice of cucumber, thin wedge of tomato, etc.

———— ◆ ————

Quick Appetizer Idea #4: Seafood pâté—Blend a can of tuna or crab meat with an equal amount of cream or cottage cheese; season with chili sauce, minced onion, parsley, celery or scallions to taste; pop in the freezer for

a few minutes to firm the mixture.
Serve with crackers for cocktails or a buffet; for a dinner, divide into servings and place each on a slice of pineapple nested in a lettuce leaf.

Quick Entrée Idea #1: Heat frozen meatballs, cooked sausage pieces, or leftover cubed chicken in spaghetti sauce and serve over pasta.

———————◆———————

Quick Entrée Idea #2: Mix in a baking dish, spaghetti sauce, shredded cheese (cheddar, mozzarella, colby, Parmesan or a mixture), one cup milk, one or two lightly beaten eggs, a dash of nutmeg, and about half as much uncooked shell or elbow macaroni as other ingredients.
Bake, covered, about 40 minutes in a 350° oven.
The dish is done when the pasta is cooked.
Serve with garlic bread and a garnish of parsley or fresh tomato wedges.

———————◆———————

Quick Entrée Idea #3: Add some shredded cheese to canned chili and heat in a low oven. Most canned chili can be extended with a can of kidney, pinto, or navy beans and some fresh or canned tomatoes without any loss of flavor.
Serve over rice with chopped onion, scallions, sour cream, and nacho chips on the side.
Or serve with a mound of nacho chips for a fast Mexican appetizer.

Quick Entrée Idea #4: Toss just–cooked and drained past in a frying pan with butter, cream and Parmesan cheese allow to thicken, adding more cheese if necessary season with salt and pepper.

Serve with a green vegetable to give the plate som color.

———————◆———————

Quick Entrée Idea #5: Same as #4; while cooking, add minced parsley and scallions, leftover vegetables o meat, etc.

———————◆———————

Quick Dessert Idea #1: A slice of frozen pound cake topped with ice cream, fruit, syrup, etc.

———————◆———————

Quick Dessert Idea #2: Heat fresh or frozen berries in a fry pan with sugar to taste; add a little rum or fruit liqueu and allow the alcohol to boil off.

Serve hot over ice cream or pound cake.

———————◆———————

Quick Dessert Idea #3: Slice an orange into attractive slices; arrange on a platter with pecan or walnut halves.

Pancakes can be the center of attraction for a simple festive brunch or dinner. If you want to serve sausage with them, place links in a pan with a little water and cook them in a moderate oven. If you check from time to time to be sure that the water doesn't cook off, this method is quite forgiving. Once the sausages are cooked turn down the oven just to keep them warm.

Pancakes can be made ahead as well and held in a warm oven, covered with a damp towel.

Years ago we regularly attended an informal gathering where some pancakes were made ahead and our host took special orders for others, allowing guests to select from a collection of ingredients such as fruit, chopped nuts, and chocolate chips. He simply poured the batter onto the griddle and placed the requested additions on top, allowing them to sink into the batter as the first side of the pancake cooked.

———— ◆ ————

To add a touch of elegance to a pancake meal, heat marmalades and fruit sections as well as syrups for topping in the microwave. Place them in a pan of hot water for serving and lay a folded towel beside the pan for catching any drips.

———— ◆ ————

Keep a list of food and guests each time you entertain. Whether your dinner parties are spur of the moment or carefully planned in advance, you may want to avoid serving the same food to the same guests, or you may want to remember which dishes made a hit.

———— ◆ ————

Planning is the key for a successful formal dinner. Make a list of the menu, decorations, and any other details so that nothing is forgotten.

Select dishes that can be prepared ahead so as to give you time to enjoy your company.

———— ◆ ————

Prepare a shopping list to make sure that everything you need is in season and available.

———— ◆ ————

Check serving pieces ahead of time to be sure that you have all you need and they are ready to use. If you need to determine the capacity of a container, use a measuring cup to fill it with water.

———— ◆ ————

Lay out serving pieces and flatware before guests arrive We often do this a day ahead of time and place a note in each piece as a reminder of what we plan to put in it Saves confusion at the last minute when we have a lot of other things on our minds.
This is especially helpful if you are taking food to someone else's party; it gives you an opportunity to figure out how to transport it without messing up the car and delivering a dish that still looks great.

———— ◆ ————

Set up decorations on a buffet table along with the serving pieces far enough ahead to allow time for a critical look and final adjustments.

———— ◆ ————

In a pinch, use a sheet for a tablecloth. With a little careful folding and taping to adjust the corners after the sheet is on the table, no one will be the wiser.

ENTERTAINING

Make a list of the things that should be set out early in order to be at room temperature when the party starts, such as butter or cheese.
Make another list of things that you want to have out when guests arrive, but that need to go out at the last minute, such as ice or chilled wine.
It's easy to forget something prepared earlier and put in the refrigerator or freezer.

———— ◆ ————

You can heat plates in the dishwasher on the drying cycle or in the oven after it is turned off.

———— ◆ ————

If you are entertaining friends who want to help, lay out serving pieces so that they can help serve. Decide ahead of time where the dirty dishes will go and let your helper stack them in the sink or the dishwasher.
Keep a spatula handy for scraping dirty dishes.

———— ◆ ————

Utensils for a buffet can be placed, handles up, in a basket or bowl lined with a cloth napkin.

———— ◆ ————

Avoid foods that need to be cut if you are not going to sit around a table to eat. It's less awkward if everything can be managed with the fingers or a fork.

———— ◆ ————

To keep food such as dip cool on a buffet, place a bowl of the food in a larger bowl containing ice, or place several bowls in a deep tray of crushed or shaved ice.

Keep cold beverages on ice in the sink— the drain will assure that the drinks are chilling on ice and not in a pool of water.

———— ◆ ————

Use a thin blanket for a table pad under a tablecloth.

———— ◆ ————

Decorate a buffet or dining table with a scattering of pine cones or fir boughs. Ivy leaves or flower petals also make an attractive decoration.

———— ◆ ————

If you are serving an attractive salad or dessert, use it as a centerpiece on the table. A bowl of fruit also works well.

———— ◆ ————

Being a good host doesn't end in the kitchen and dining room... Be sure the bathroom is well-stocked with necessities such as toilet paper, soap, and hand towels. Add a pleasant touch by lighting a couple of candles in large holders that assure they won't become a fire hazard.

Cleaning Tips

Some Words of Caution:

DO NOT MIX CHLORINE BLEACH AND AMMONIA.
The two liquids can combine to form an odorless, colorless gas that can be lethal and in a confined space may be explosive.

A GREAT RULE OF THUMB is to keep only one of the cleaners in the house. We mostly use chlorine bleach, so that's the one we keep around; for those occasional project that call for ammonia we buy a small amount, use what we need, and discard the rest.

READ PRODUCT LABELS. Some cleansers contain chlorine bleach; other detergents and glass cleaners contain ammonia—as noted above, the two must never be mixed.
Pay special attention to the WARNING label: it's not limited to suggesting that the cleaner should not be used as a food or beverage. (Is there anyone who can read who

doesn't already know that?) The label will also contain information about such things as caustic ingredients and types of surfaces that might be harmed by contact with the cleaner, including your skin!

DO NOT USE AMMONIA CLEANERS ON VARNISHED SURFACES. Ammonia can soften the varnish, causing ripples that will mar the smooth surface.

ALWAYS TEST FABRICS, PAINTED SURFACES, ETC. before using a new cleaner to be sure that it will not damage the material.

Cleaning Techniques

To save steps, put together a carrier with your most commonly used cleaners and cleaning tools. Inexpensive plastic totes designed to hold tools or cleaners are readily available on the market, or you may want to use a wash bucket or tray to carry your supplies.

Some of us keep a separate box or tray containing all of our cleaning products and tools under the sink along with the carrier. Then when we take on a project, we just load the carrier up with the stuff we need. The box or tray is also easy to remove when we want to clean under the sink.

To save time, keep paper towels or cleaning cloths, glass cleaner, tile cleaner, toilet bowl cleaner, and brushes in each bathroom for 'as needed' cleanups.

Recycle old bath towels. Cut them up to use for cleaning rags or to wipe your hands when you are cleaning, then wash and reuse them. Not only do you save on paper towels, but cloth rags often do a better job.
Note: If you don't hem the rags, wash them separately or they will pass lint on to everything else in the laundry.

Fold and stack clean cloths and keep a bag or bucket handy for used cloths; that way you won't accidentally use a cloth that is dirty or has the wrong cleaner on it.

Clean the cleaning tools and rags often to avoid spreading germs and dirt.

Cloths that are to be used repeatedly, such as one for buffing furniture, can be kept handy by securing them to the container of cleaner or polish with a rubber band.

Use paper toweling for messy jobs that can ruin cleaning rags, but keep in mind that they are not nearly as good as

terry or soft cotton such as old diapers for most jobs.
Paper towels can scratch Plexiglas, glasses with plastic lenses, tinted windows, the kitchen range hood, or any painted surface that gets wiped often.

Save that old toothbrush! First, clean and disinfect the toothbrush by soaking it in a glass of water containing a teaspoonful of bleach.
An old toothbrush is great for getting into tight spaces or cleaning intricate objects such as fancy hinges or drawer pulls.

Keep a small laundry basket handy to save steps. Items that don't belong in the room you're cleaning can be put in the basket to be returned to their proper places later.

Have the kids outgrown their old doll buggy? It's small enough to hang in the laundry room for storage and is ideal for collecting odd items that can be matched up or redistributed later.

Make a handy utility broom that will fit in your work basket. Simply cut down the handle and trim the bristles of an old or out of shape broom.

CLEANING TIPS

A kangaroo apron—one with pockets—is helpful for holding small objects you pick up around the house that need to be put away later. It's convenient for keeping a dust cloth near at hand as well.

Keep a project basket to hold things that need attention later such as a cracked vase that needs to be glued or an article of clothing in need of a button.
Don't get sidetracked when you find photos that should go in the family album; by just put them in the project basket to be dealt with later.

Surfaces are much easier to maintain if they are free of clutter. Keep seldom–used items in drawers or cabinets. Organize essential items that must be left out on trays or in baskets that are easy to move for cleaning.

Recycle your cleaning materials whenever possible. Baking soda that has been used to soak up odors in the refrigerator, for example, can still be used as a cleaner. Old, ratty cleaning cloths can be handy for mopping up messy spills or stains, then tossed out.

When tackling the whole house, make a schedule and do your best to stick to it so that you don't get sidetracked or bogged down with a few chores. Setting a time limit for each room and using a timer to go off five or ten minutes

before the time is up will give you the choice of finishing quickly or putting off the next room to another day.
If you consistently run out of time, you'll eventually learn how you can modify the schedule or your methods in the future.

Clean around a room one wall at a time, working systematically from top to bottom in order to avoid missing an area.

A thorough cleaning with the proper tools lasts longer than a quick once over and can give one a real sense of accomplishment.

Dust surfaces before washing them to remove loose dirt that will muddy up your cleaning solution.

Use all cleaning products with care. Avoid creating extra work by damaging the surrounding area with overspray or splashes.

When using any cleaner, moisten cloth with the cleaning solution and blot or rub gently, cleaning a small area at a time; then rinse well.

CLEANING TIPS

Wipe surfaces thoroughly and methodically. Be sure to get the corners, edges, splash guards, backboards, etc. Work in a regular pattern to make certain you get it all.

When working in the bathroom or kitchen, carefully clean the underside of the water faucet and around the edges of the drain and overflow, damp places where mold and mildew get their start. Rinse brushes, rags, and the sink well to avoid further distributing the spores that can spread mold and mildew.

Use a coaster, newspaper, or plastic lid for setting a container of cleaner on to avoid marking surfaces.
Liquid floor wax is especially good at getting stuck where it's not supposed to be because a few drops always seem to want to dribble down the side of the container just when you decide to rest it somewhere.

If you don't have a coaster, place the container of cleaner in your carrier or bucket when you have to set it down.

To thoroughly clean a cluttered area, remove everything from the area, then clean and dust items as you replace them.

Before you vacuum, use a broom to brush dirt away from the corners and edges of the room and furniture.

To thoroughly get up the dirt around the edges, just circle the room with the long upholstery nozzle. Vacuum the baseboards with the brush attachment.

Whatever the area you are cleaning, the more thorough you are, the longer it will remain clean.

Shining the glass on pictures, kitchen faucets and counter tops makes any room look finished. And don't forget to polish the drawer pulls and door knobs.

When moving heavy furniture or appliances to clean around them, tilt them first and slide a flattened cardboard carton under the front or side. You can then tilt the other way to shift the load and slide the object easily with the help of the cardboard and without scratching or marring the floor.

Use unprinted newsprint stock for a variety of chores around the house, particularly to cover areas you want to protect when cleaning or painting. Most local newspapers will give you their stub rolls free, although they may require a deposit for the core on which the paper is wound.

Most cleaners are much the same; only the names change. Most of the time, all you need is something to moisten and dissolve grease and dirt; soap and water still works best with occasional additives for special jobs.

Expensive abrasive cleaners can be a waste of money. Many scrubbing jobs can be done quite nicely with baking soda and vinegar at a fraction of the cost.

Save odd socks for dusting. Use one as a hand mitt or secure several to a broom handle with rubber bands to reach out of the way places.

Allow gentler cleaners to work while you do other things. Many of our tips call for a treatment to rest for a few minutes, an hour, or even overnight, allowing *TIME* to do most of the work.

It's easier to allow a pan to soak in soapy water while you wipe down the stove rather than scrubbing or scraping it immediately.

Ease the cleanup after cooking by rinsing and stacking dishes and pans as you go. This is especially important for food that can harden and create a major chore later. Pans with dried egg on them, for example, need to be soaked in cold water. Hot water hardens the egg.

Cleaning with Vinegar

To get rid of grease marks on glass, wipe with water to which a little vinegar has been added and rinse well.

White vinegar removes mustard, wax and jelly stains. Vinegar is safe for most fibers, but as with all cleaners, it should be first tested to be sure the dye in the fabric is colorfast.

Clean stains from non–stick pans by boiling a mixture of water, four tablespoons vinegar and one tablespoon baking soda for about ten minutes.

To remove lime deposits from cookware, bring a solution of one–third vinegar and two–thirds water to a boil and let it stand in the pan overnight.

Mineral deposits tend to build up on containers used

regularly for heating water. Rinse them out occasionally and give them the vinegar treatment. That grayish coating on the inside of the teakettle can make your tea bitter and may eventually chip off.

Use vinegar in the bath to kill fungi that can cause athlete's foot and other skin diseases.

Vinegar stops the action of bleach! To reduce the damage of a spill, dab on vinegar with a cloth or sponge as quickly as possible.

Grass stains may be removed with a mixture of one part vinegar to two parts water; dab on and blot dry.

Mineral deposits from hard water can quickly clog a shower head. To clear the deposits from a metal head, remove it and boil in a solution of ½ cup of vinegar to one quart of water.
Plastic shower heads can be cleaned by soaking for a longer period in the same solution which should be hot, but off the heat.

Vinegar will remove toilet bowl stains. Just pour a cup of vinegar in the bowl and allow it to stand overnight. It will soak up odors as well.

Cleaning with Ammonia

Ammonia is a harsh alkaline cleaner that can discolor fabric and some plastics such as padded toilet seat covers; it can darken metal and dissolve varnish.

Ammonia is effective for removing wax buildup on floors, but it can attack the finish. Don't use ammonia full strength over a large area and we don't recommend using it on varnished floors at all.

Always wear gloves when cleaning with ammonia; it is ammonia in urine that gives babies diaper rash.

When cleaning with ammonia, use plain rather than scented, as the additives reduce the cleaning power.

CLEANING TIPS

For quick cleanups of non–porous surfaces, use equal parts ammonia and water. Rub on with a sponge, rinse well, and rub surface dry.
Rubbing a surface dry will bring out the shine.

Glass containers can be cleaned quickly with a mixture of one teaspoonful of ammonia and one cup of water. Rinse well and polish with a soft cloth.

Remove grime from windows by washing with a teaspoonful of ammonia added to a cup of water; dry immediately after cleaning. Once dry, use a fresh cloth or paper to go over the surface one more time to polish it.
We like terry toweling best for drying and shining, but old newspapers also do a wonderful job.

Use ammonia to restore articles stained by smoke, such as glassware, mirrors, Formica, and straw or wicker.

Easy oven cleaning is a matter of timing. Place a glass dish containing about ¼ cup of ammonia in the oven and leave overnight.
Next morning, remove the dish and add the remaining ammonia to four cups of water. Remove racks, place them in the sink, and wipe them down with the ammonia mixture. Rinse well and rub them dry. Sponge off the

oven walls with the ammonia mixture. Work on any crusted areas with a scrubby, then rinse, and wipe dry.
If stains persist in the oven and on the shelves, repeat.
If you leave the ammonia in the oven for two or three days, the odor will spread throughout the kitchen. Overnight, it's hardly noticeable.
Follow the same technique with commercial cleaners— don't waste your time and energy scrubbing, let *time* alone do most of the work.

When you clean the oven, put the pans from under the burners in the oven as well.

Leave a note when you clean the oven. A note taped to the oven door will alert others (and, perhaps you) that cleaning is in process so that no one cooks your cleaner.

If you damage a varnished surface with ammonia, try applying a thin coat of liquid floor wax to restore the texture and shine. If the first coat is uneven because the wax is soaking in, reapply. If necessary, apply several light coats; above all, don't try to apply a single heavy coat.

To smooth a varnished surface roughened by ammonia or other chemicals, try rubbing lightly with 0000 grade steel wool, but be careful to lightly hit the high spots only: you don't want to cut through the remaining varnish.

Cleaning with Bleach

Remove stains from plastic or glass, such as those from iced tea left in a pitcher, by soaking for a few minutes in warm water to which a few tablespoons of bleach have been added. When the stain is gone, rinse well.

Chlorine bleach in water is still the best method of getting rid of black mold and mildew.

To your collection of cleaners, add a spray bottle of bleach water—about one tablespoon of bleach to a pint of water should do it—and keep it handy for spraying tiles, shower curtains, and other places where black mold and mildew form.

Once mold has been allowed to form, you've got it. It thrives in a moist, warm, dark environment. As a preventive measure, regularly spray the grouting and caulking around tub and shower tiles. Avoid using straight bleach or harsh cleansers that can damage the surface of grout, making it even more susceptible to subsequent attacks.

Sanitize the dishes with a tablespoonful of chlorine bleach added to the wash or rinse water.

Keep the dishwasher free of mildew and germs between uses by adding a tablespoonful of chlorine bleach each time you wash dishes.

Chrome handles and trim can be damaged by excess exposure to chlorine bleach.

Cleaning with Baking Soda

Clean kitchen and bathroom tiles, and counter tops with baking soda. Sprinkle a little baking soda on a wet cloth or sponge, scrub, rinse, and polish dry.

Replace those abrasive cleaners with baking soda. Use baking soda, as noted above, anywhere that you would normally use abrasive cleaners.

Freshen laundry by adding about one–fourth cup of baking soda along with your regular detergent.

Burnt pots and pans come clean when you sprinkle them with a coating of baking soda, moisten and allow to stand overnight.

To remove coffee, tea or cigarette stains from china, rub with a damp cloth dipped in baking soda.

Cleaning with Alcohol

Clean to the shine with rubbing alcohol! Most finished surfaces have a built-in shine, often dulled by dust and grease from the air; before using wax or polish, try using alcohol to cut through the grease—you may not need the wax.

Plain candles are easily cleaned with a rag that has been moistened with rubbing alcohol. If the candle has a painted or appliquéd design, test first to be sure that the alcohol doesn't attack it.

Clean window sills and frames with alcohol for a finish that sparkles.

Water spots on stainless steel can be removed by wiping with alcohol.

To make windows sparkle clean them with a mixture of two tablespoons of alcohol and two quarts of water. Dry completely with crumpled newspaper.

Television and computer screens are magnets for dust. Be sure to turn them off before cleaning, then wipe with a lint–free cloth dampened with alcohol. The alcohol will evaporated quickly, preventing any liquid from seeping into the equipment.

Clean computer cabinets and keyboards with alcohol as well. Alcohol will cut through the oily residue left by your hands or the air and its quick evaporation will prevent any damage to the electronics.

Miscellaneous Cleaning Tips

To remove candle wax from a carpet, fabric, or a counter top, cover area with a paper towel and press down with a warm iron (no steam). The toweling will absorb the melted wax and a clean towel will remove any residue from the iron. Be sure to test fabric to make sure the heat of the iron will not damage it.

Change the toweling as needed to absorb all the wax. Wipe down the iron while still warm, making sure that there is no wax in the steam vents.

It's easier to remove wax from a candle holder if you freeze it first. Most of the wax will chip off.

To remove stubborn wax from a candle holder, dip it in very hot water. Sometimes the wax will melt and float off; at other times you have to soak it up with a paper towel. After most of the wax is gone, give the holder a final dip in the water and wipe it dry with a paper towel. Repeat if any smears remain.

An old toothbrush can be used to clear the wax from filigree work that you can't reach with the paper towel.

HANDY HOUSEHOLD HINTS

Clean eyeglasses with a few drops of vodka.

When cleaning with lemon, after squeezing out the juice, turn the lemon half inside out to use as an applicator. Once the job is done, run the lemon through the garbage disposal to freshen it.

Remove rust from garden tools with steel wool dipped in kerosene or turpentine. Then oil the tools lightly to prevent the rust from forming again.

Clean stains from non–stick pans by boiling a mixture of water, four tablespoons vinegar and one tablespoon baking soda for about ten minutes.

To clean a stubborn stain from a marble counter or table top, cover with a folded paper towel that has been wet with full strength hydrogen peroxide. Cover with a sheet of plastic wrap, weigh down with a book or other heavy object, and check in an hour or two. If stain is not gone, continue process.

Make that old refrigerator shine with a coat of automobile paste wax applied according to the directions on the can. The next cleaning will be easier, too.

CLEANING TIPS

To whiten old appliances, mix a half cup of bleach, a quarter cup of baking soda and four cups of warm water. Apply with a sponge and allow to remain for ten minutes. Then rinse and dry thoroughly.

After an oven spill, immediately sprinkle with salt. When oven cools, brush off burnt food and collect ashes in toweling. Wipe clean.

Remove water spots from stainless steel by wiping with white vinegar and drying well.

To restore the shine to an aluminum pan, fill the pan with water, add a couple of tablespoons of cream of tartar or vinegar and boil for a few minutes.

Water can ruin a wooden cutting board or chopping block. Don't allow it to soak in water and do stand it on edge to dry out thoroughly after washing.

Easy cleanup for a broiler pan or barbecue grill—sprinkle with dry laundry detergent, then cover with a damp cloth or paper towel. The pan or grill should come clean with little scouring.

To remove cooked on food from a casserole dish, fill the dish with boiling water and add two teaspoons of baking soda or table salt. Allow to soak and rinse clean.

To clean copper, mix three tablespoons of salt with one and one–half cups of vinegar. Spray liberally on copper, let it set, then rub clean and polish.

Clean burnt pans by boiling two cups of water and half a cup of oatmeal for five minutes, stirring as it comes to a boil. Cover, remove from heat and allow to stand overnight. The oatmeal will absorb the burned on particles.

Polish with toothpaste! Clean and polish a high gloss surface by rubbing with toothpaste, letting it dry, and then buffing to a nice shine.

To clean the barbecue grill, cover the top of the grill with aluminum foil and wrap tightly at the edges. Just before cooking, when the coals are hottest, place the grill over the fire and "cook" it for about ten minutes. Remove the foil and any residue will brush off easily.

CLEANING TIPS

Use coffee to clean a griddle! Works for frying pans, too. Just pour coffee over the griddle or pan and wipe it off.

When you spatter liquid shoe polish on the bathroom sink, pour a little flat beer over it. The polish comes right off even after it has dried.

Use liquid furniture polish to clean the range hood. It won't harm the finish and it leaves a nice shine.

Roach proof your home or apartment with a treatment of boric acid purchased from any pharmacy. Use a squeeze bottle, bulb baster or a container with holes in the lid to sprinkle over cracks and crevices in pantry shelves, in kitchen and bathroom drawers, around major appliances, under sinks and around baseboards.

In cases of heavy infestation, it may take a few days before the treatment will make a difference, but once it takes hold, the creatures disappear completely. It is necessary to repeat the treatment only once or twice a year unless there is evidence of new activity, in which case apply to the area as necessary.

Make your own roach motel. For an area where a general application of boric acid is not practical, mix boric acid with sugar, jelly or catsup and carefully place in the outer wrap of a small wooden match box, a bottle cap, or a jar lid. Replace every thirty days or so.

Clean window and door screens by dusting both sides with a brush, then brushing with kerosene and wiping dry.

When cleaning up broken glass use wet paper towels or napkins to wipe up the small pieces and slivers.

When you use rubber gloves for cleaning, sprinkle a little talcum powder on your hands to make it easier to get the gloves off and on.

Leaky spray bottle? Wrap a strip of old toweling around the container and secure it with a rubber band to catch pesky drips.

Most painted or papered walls can be washed with water and a mild detergent, but test in an inconspicuous place first. Not all paints and papers are washable and even those that are may be attacked by some cleaners, especially those containing ammonia or bleach.

CLEANING TIPS

When washing painted or papered walls, work from bottom to top to avoid streaks from drips.

Wash walls with the least amount of water possible and work a small area at a time.

Spots on most non–washable walls can be cleaned with a soft art gum eraser, available at art stores.

Before using a cleaner on a metal lamp or decorative object, be sure that it is not coated with a protective film that can be damaged by the cleaner. If you lack manufacturer's instructions, test first.

Restore the shine to brass objects with 0000 grade steel wool. Test first to be sure that the brass is not just a coating that can be removed by the wool.

To clean plastic plug or switch plates, remove them and soak in water to which a small amount of chlorine bleach has been added. They will usually rinse clean after about thirty minutes

When you need heavy duty soap to clean your hands, try using that laundry pre–wash spray.

Make your own hand cleaner by mixing equal parts of baking soda, dry laundry detergent and corn meal.
This kind of rough treatment isn't especially good for your hands, however, so we recommend using plastic gloves for really messy tasks.

To wash venetian blinds, wear cloth gloves moistened with the cleaning solution. Just dip the gloves in water with a bit of vinegar or detergent added and wring out. Your hands will mold to the blinds better than any brush or plain cloth.

For easier cleaning of venetian blinds, hang them over the bathtub or outside. Then you can rinse them with the shower or garden hose.

Brighten the tape and strings on venetian blinds with white shoe polish.

Rub venetian blinds with a coat of liquid wax to make the next cleaning easier. All you have to do is wipe them with a dry cloth to make them dazzle again.

Make a floor wax applicator from a short–napped or sponge paint roller. Get the type of roller handle that accepts a screw–type mop handle extension so you don't have to bend.

This is especially effective for large areas such as a family room, or for a room with textured floors.

Dust can destroy carpets, upholstery and linens if it contains chemical residue and is allowed to remain on the article for an extended period.

Dust is also abrasive and can ruin the finish on furniture and floors as well as collectibles.

Dust with a soft cloth and a spray that will trap dust in the cloth and minimize abrasion. Work slowly and systematically, turning the cloth inward as the outer surface becomes soiled.

Clean gilded picture frames with beer. Dip a soft cloth in beer and wipe. Blot moisture out of crevices in intricately carved frames with a soft cloth.

To get rid of snails or slugs, place a glass or can in a hole so that the top is level with the ground, fill almost to the rim with beer and leave overnight. In the morning, dump the drowned pests on the compost heap.

Clean rubber heel marks from kitchen linoleum with a moist cloth dabbed in floor wax. The marks will usually come up without leaving a dull spot.

Keep wooden drawers and their contents dry by placing the small drying packets that come in coffee and other products in them.

To brighten old porcelain, try rubbing with a solution of salt dissolved in turpentine. Rinse and polish with a soft cloth.

Clean badly stained porcelain with a paste of peroxide and cream of tartar. Simply scrub with a brush and rinse. If the stain persists, try again by covering the stain with the paste and allowing it to stand for one to two hours, then scrub and rinse.

Stains on old porcelain can be helped with a bar of Fels Naptha or Octagon soap dissolved in one gallon of hot water with half a cup of mineral spirits added. Brush vig-

orously on the surface.
NOTE: Be sure that the "stain" isn't just the metal show-
ing through a layer of porcelain worn thin before you
brush with anything too coarse.

To shine the walls around a shower, apply an automobile
paste wax and buff it, following directions on the can.
Dry the tiles after each shower and the shine will last for
months.

**Tiles in the shower stall are easiest to clean immediately
after someone has showered**—the steam loosens the dirt!
Taking a minute to wipe down the walls after a shower
can save a lot of work (and expensive cleaners) later.

To prevent mildew be sure to spread the curtain open after
taking a shower.

If the shower curtain mildews at the bottom it's probably
because it is allowed to rest against the bottom or side of
the tub. Try to reposition the bar so that the curtain can
hang loose and dry between uses.

To clean ceramic tile, mix two tablespoons of tri–sodium phosphate, available from the hardware store, in one gallon of water.

To clear rust stains caused by a can, razor or bobby pin left on the edge of tub or sink, rub with a paste of borax and lemon juice. Allow to dry, then brush away the stain with the powder.

Clear those drains and save the cost of a plumber. Use a paper towel to remove hairs and other debris caught in the bathroom and kitchen drains before they slide down and cause a clog.

Clean drains occasionally with one cup of baking soda and one cup of vinegar. Allow it to foam briefly, then pour in a few cups of boiling water.

To brighten bathroom fixtures, rub with a cloth dampened in kerosene. The kerosene not only removes scum from the fixtures, it is also an inexpensive way to do so.

When cleaning the bathroom, check behind the door! The molding and area behind the door are often ignored, and retain dirt and germs that are quickly spread around the rest of the room.

To keep the toilet clean, those blue treatments really do a good job, but check the label—some contain bleach that will eventually corrode the metal parts of the flush mechanism.

Dry clean artificial flowers by shaking them in a paper bag with a cup of salt.

Some artificial flowers are washable! Dip the flowers, one at a time, in a solution of two tablespoons of sudsy ammonia and one quart of water, rinse well, and drain on towels.

Silk flowers can be cleaned with a solution of warm water and white vinegar. Some colors may fade, so dip them individually after blowing or vacuuming off loose dirt.

Brighten the carpets with cornstarch! Sprinkle cornstarch generously on the carpet and allow to stand for about one hour before vacuuming.

Removing fresh mud from carpeting is easy with cornstarch. Sprinkle cornstarch over the mud, allow it to dry, then vacuum away the mud with the cornstarch.

Resist the urge to work the cornstarch into the carpet—let it absorb the moisture slowly and naturally. Repeat as necessary to remove all of the wet mud.

Clean oil stains from a concrete drive or garage by covering with mineral spirits and allowing to soak for thirty minutes to one hour. Scrub with a stiff brush, adding more mineral spirits if necessary. Wipe with toweling, wash with detergent, and rinse well.

Dry a concrete floor easily with a squeegee attached to a mop handle. If there's no drain, use a dust pan to collect the liquid and put it in a bucket.

Clean small-necked vases with a bottle brush. You can find the brushes in the baby section of a food store.

To clean a glass flower vase, use toilet bowl cleaner, allow to stand for ten minutes and rinse well.

CLEANING TIPS

Catch streaks when cleaning windows, by using an up and down stroke on one side and side to side stroke on the other; when you see streaks you know which side they are on.

Add life to carpeting by keeping throw rugs in doorways. Most wear occurs at the edge of the carpet. Makes cleaning easier, too.

When waxing or polishing with steel wool, ALWAYS rub with the grain.
Wipe up residue and check your progress frequently—a little polishing can go a long way.

To revive a counter top worn by time and cleaners try applying a thin coat of liquid floor wax or auto wax.

Remove tape, labels or their gummy residue from glass by wetting them and scraping with a wet razor blade. The water helps avoid scratches on the glass.

To clean those copper pans, wet the bottom and sprinkle with salt to coat completely. Allow to rest for a few minutes and rinse. Resist the urge to scrub.

Controlling Odors

**It used to be called 'housatosis', a house's bad breath.
Odors may seem merely unpleasant,
but they can signal the formation of harmful bacteria.**

A major step to controlling odors is to identify them in order to eliminate their source:

- **Moldy or Musty Odor**—Check for leaks under sinks, behind toilets and around fixtures in the sinks. Check flooring or carpet around the base of the tub for moisture after a shower or bath. Check around the base of outside doors, especially after a rain. (Sliding glass doors are most likely culprits.)
- **Grease or Food Odor**—Clean garbage cans inside and out. Check under the range top and around stove knobs. Clean the range hood and fan filter. Check the oven—it's best to clean spills before they burn on.

Mold stinks—mold spreads—mold stains—and many people have an allergic reaction to mold. Mold is influenced by:

- Moisture—It loves it!
- Heat—It thrives in moist heat!

• Darkness—Mold doesn't need light. Bathroom mold will climb up the wall and fill a dark shower enclosure in an amazingly short time.

By the time mold is visible it is well on the way to being out of control in which case you will have to scrub the grout as well as the tiles. Use a small stiff brush and be sure to include the bottom edges of the tiles where they meet the tub and all of the caulking around the tub.

Commercial sprays that can kill mold will most likely contain chlorine bleach; for your own mix, use 1 part bleach to 3 parts water. Spray the entire area, allow the mixture to remain for a few minutes. Air out the room, then rinse and wipe dry. When mold has begun to spread you have to be meticulous about cleaning up behind it. Respray a light misting of the bleach solution on the cleaned area and allow to dry naturally.

To freshen and remove odors from storage bottles and jars, allow them to stand for a few hours with a mixture of water and a little dry mustard.

To quickly clear the air in a room of smoke, wet a towel and wring it out, then wave it briskly through the air.

To cut down on cigarette smoke in the air, burn candles.

To keep closets fresh and free of moths sprinkle cedar chips along the back and sides of the floor and shelves, or place the chips in an old stocking and hang it in an out of the way place.

For a pleasant smell in your home, poke holes with an ice pick in a thin–skinned juice orange and stud it with whole cloves, then roll in powdered cinnamon. Hang the orange by a ribbon near a doorway, or place several in a bowl to add spicy fragrance to a room.

Eventually, the fruit will dry out and last for years. Once dry, it can be placed in a dresser drawer to scent it.

Fill a shallow container with potpourri and slide it under a sofa or large chair. Pull it out and 'fluff' it up from time to time; change it or add scented oil when the fragrance dissipates.

Clean under sofa or chair cushions regularly to remove lint and debris.

Air out the cushions. We take cushions, throw pillows, lap robe, etc. outside and shake them out. Bang them together to free them of dust and lint, then lay them out on the patio furniture to air. Use a small stiff brush to get rid of debris around buttons and seams.

CONTROLLING ODORS

Living room drapes should be vacuumed often, paying special attention to the tops (look for cobwebs) and bottoms (pet hair).

Be sure the vacuum head is clean—most can be washed with soap and water—before tackling the drapes. No sense leaving residue behind when you are trying to clean.

If the vacuum cleaner emits a bad smell, something is wrong.

- **Have you vacuumed over a wet area?** Wet material in the confines of the vacuum cleaner bag can take on a life of its own in just a few days.
- **Is the bag old?** Sometimes when areas aren't too dirty it seems that the bag will last forever, but it won't... The *time* that nasty stuff has been in the bag can be as important as the *amount* in the bag. Even a small amount of material will develop an aroma over time.
- **Are the utensils clean?** Bits of grease and dust that stick to the housing, brush, and roller can cause odors that are recirculated every time you vacuum. Clean them well for best results.
- **When there is a pervasive odor** that just won't go away in spite of all your efforts, try inserting a dryer sheet inside between the outer bag or casing and the disposable bag. If that doesn't work, the only recourse is to remove the disposable bag and wipe down the machine inside and out with a cloth dampened in a mixture of bleach or vinegar and water.

Change the vacuum cleaner bag after vacuuming behind a pet. Of course the little darling is beautiful, but the hair contains oil and debris that can create an odoriferous nuisance.

Add lemon peel to cleaning water for a pleasant smell.

To get rid of pet odors in your pet's favorite resting place, scrub a mixture of white vinegar and water into the carpet, then sponge with club soda.

Gather up the pet's bedding carefully so as to contain any hair, dander, parasite eggs, etc. Wash in the hottest water possible with plenty of soap. Rinse well—we are inclined to run through the rinse cycle twice so as to eliminate any chance of soap residue that will irritate the pet.
Take extra care to clean out the washer and dryer filters after drying the bedding as well.

Even the pet's bed needs laundering. Use the bath tub or a pet washing tub to soak a cat's basket in a mixture of warm water and mild soap for a few minutes. Brush well to remove hair and dirt; rinse with a vinegar and water mixture. Allow to dry thoroughly in the sun.

CONTROLLING ODORS

To get rid of carpet odors, add one box of baking soda to three boxes of cornstarch and sprinkle on the carpet. Allow to rest for a few minutes before vacuuming.

Keep the litter box fresh longer with a generous sprinkling of baking soda.

To dispel strong odors such as smoke, leave an open dish of vinegar in the room.

Clean ashtrays regularly. Empty them into a small paper or plastic bag and close tightly before depositing in a waste basket. Wash the ashtrays with soap and water frequently to remove all trace of stale ashes and tar.

To get rid of stale or dusty odors:
- Open windows to air out the house on a regular basis.
- Vacuum draperies and valances.
- Dust the ledge over doorways and windows.
- Clean mini–blinds.
- Wipe windowsills.
- Dust and clean window screens.
- Change the heater and air conditioner filters.
- Clean carpets.
- Wash throw rugs and bath mats.
- Air out area rugs.

Keep towels and linens fresh by keeping potpourri in the cupboard or drawer where they are kept.

Make your own air freshener by mixing one cup of alcohol with one cup of water and adding a few drops of concentrated potpourri scent.
Keep the mixture handy in a spray bottle and use just as you would an aerosol deodorant.

Controlling Kitchen Odors

Cover unpleasant odors with appetizing ones. Onions frying in butter will mask almost any other cooking odor. Even if you don't need onions right away, cooked onions will keep in the refrigerator for several days and can be added to prepared foods such as green beans, sauerkraut, or spaghetti sauce to impart a homemade flavor.

Pop a batch of popcorn! It's inexpensive, easy to make, smells great, and makes a good snack for people or birds.

To remove odors from a cutting board after cutting onions, garlic, or fish, rub salt on the board, let sit for a couple of minutes, and rinse.

Cutting board odors can also be removed by rubbing the board with a slice of lemon or lime, then rinsing well.

Eliminate musty refrigerator odors by placing a small open box of baking soda in the refrigerator and in the freezer. Replace every thirty to sixty days; the old soda can be used as a light scouring powder.

Check the drip pan under the refrigerator. Remove and clean the grill at the bottom front of the refrigerator. Pull out the tray, empty it, and wash well.
Note: Unplug the refrigerator before you mess around down there. You have to pull the refrigerator out to unplug it, so it's a good time to clean the sides and back.
Try to keep the top clean and free of clutter—it's an area that's easy to ignore because most of us can't see it.

Pour used baking soda down the drain and add a little to the strainers. Replace the strainers loosely and pour one–half cup of vinegar down the drain. (Pour down each side of a double sink.) The mixture will bubble up in the strainers to clean them as well as the pipes.

Remove fish odors from your hands by washing them in salted or lemon water.

After you extract the juice from a lemon, run the skins through the garbage disposal to freshen it. If you have more than you need to do the job, freeze the rest for use another time.

To counteract odors in the garbage disposal, add a few tablespoons of baking soda and allow it to remain until the next time you run the disposal.

To remove odors from plastic containers, stuff them with newspaper. Cover tightly and leave them overnight.

Sprinkle baking soda in a garbage or diaper pail to reduce unpleasant odors.

To keep the dishwasher fresh between uses, sprinkle a little baking soda in the bottom after emptying it.

The dishwasher needs a thorough washing at least once a year. Remove the trays and wipe down the inside walls with a soapy cloth.

Mineral deposits that dull the finish and can cause permanent damage may accumulate on the inside of the machine. Odor–causing molds can also form—nip them by rinsing with a solution of vinegar or bleach and water. Check the drain at the bottom of the machine from time to time for residual food particles that can cause odors. Clean the drain by applying a liberal sprinkling of baking soda, then pouring about half a cup of vinegar over it. When the bubbling stops, rinse well.

If kitchen appliances aren't built in, the narrow spaces between them and counter tops collect a variety of spills, dust, and debris. Pull out the appliances periodically for a good cleaning of these areas that are prime areas for breeding odors and bugs.

Disinfect door handles, drawer pulls, and appliance handles regularly with disinfecting spray, bleach water, or alcohol to limit the spread of bacteria and germs throughout the house.

Kitchen curtains can absorb and disseminate odors rather quickly—get curtains that are washable and wash them regularly.

Don't overlook curtains or drapes in an eating area. They will trap odors almost as readily as those in the kitchen.

...And don't forget the cupboards, range hood, and walls. When you fry, broil, or steam food, tiny particles carried in the air wind up on all surfaces. They smell great coming off the food, but they may not smell so great after they've been around awhile. Wipe down all surfaces including appliances on a regular basis. Go over the walls once or twice a year with vinegar and water.

Wash the kitchen garbage can regularly with soap and water. Even if you use liners, some smells linger.

Clean a cutting board with a sprinkling of baking soda. Allow the baking soda to remain for a few minutes, then rinse with plain water.

Freshen thermos bottles, coffee makers, etc. by rinsing them with warm water mixed with two to three table-spoons of baking soda.

Fresh mint and basil exude a delightful fragrance. Hang them from a nail or store them in an open basket.

Removing Spots & Stains

Attack spills carefully to prevent a stain!
- **Resist the urge to immediately use a cleaner** that can set the stain.
- **Take the time to blot up as much as possible**, working from the outer edge toward the middle. Resist rubbing. If necessary, as on a thick carpet, lay down a layer of clean paper towels or terry toweling and press or weigh them down until they get wet. Repeat the process until all of the moisture has been absorbed.
- **Use water to dilute the stain.** Carefully add water, then blot it up. Repeat until the stain is gone or it is no longer coming off with the water. Only after you've done all you can with this method is it time to consider stronger stain removal methods.

Approach fabric stains in a similar fashion:
- **Try to determine the source of the stain.**
- **Begin by using water** to soften and carry away as much residue as possible. Place an absorbent pad over the stain, then turn the material over and moisten the back with water from a damp rag. Then blot from the front with a dry clean rag. Work slowly and carefully keeping the moisture confined to the area of the stain as much as possible to avoid spreading it. Resist the urge to scrub as you could damage the fabric.
- **When residue no longer comes out with the water,** use

a cleaning agent or the suggestions outlined in this chapter.

- **Use the cleaner sparingly** to avoid spreading the stain; moisten the area with the cleaner and dab up just as you did with the water.
- **When the spot is gone** or the cleaner is no longer effective, flush with water to remove the cleaner. At this point, if the stain is not gone, you may want to repeat the procedure.
- **As a final step,** while the material is damp, rub gently outward from the edges of the wet area to blend and remove any trace of a ring left by the cleaner.

Fruit stains can be removed from hands with a mixture of lemon juice and salt. Just squirt the lemon on your hands, sprinkle on a little salt, and rub lightly. Rinse in clear water. If the stain isn't gone, repeat the process.

Use peroxide to "digest" blood and chocolate stains and the sooner applied, the better.

Place the stain face down on an absorbent pad and apply peroxide to the back. Allow peroxide to soak through to work on the stain and be absorbed by the pad on the face. Blot up bubbles formed by the action of the peroxide on the back and reapply fresh peroxide if necessary.

Dried stains may require soaking in cold water for at least an hour between treatments.

When stain is gone or peroxide treatments are no longer effective, wash in a good detergent in cold water.

Peroxide is safe for most fabrics, but should be tested first to be sure the dye is colorfast.

REMOVING SPOTS AND STAINS

To clean kitchen woodwork stained by smoke spread a paste of cornstarch and water on the woodwork and allow it to dry. Remove the dried residue with a soft brush or cloth, taking away the stain with the corn starch.

To clean a stubborn stain from a counter or table top, cover with a folded paper towel that has been wet with full strength hydrogen peroxide. Cover with a sheet of plastic wrap, weigh down with a book or other heavy object, and check in an hour or two.
If the stain is not gone, repeat the process.

Use club soda to remove fresh stains. Pour some on the spot, wait a few seconds and soak it up with a clean paper towel.

To get rid of fresh oil or other fluids from the car in the carport, driveway, or other hard surface, cover the oil with kitty litter and sweep or vacuum up after the oil is absorbed.

Corn starch will also soak up fresh oil. Sprinkle the corn starch over the area and sweep or vacuum after the oil is absorbed.

For an old oil stain on a driveway or garage floor, make a paste of laundry detergent mixed with equal parts of water and bleach. Spread the paste over the stain and allow it to stand for an hour or more; then scrub vigorously with a brush or broom. Cover with plastic if necessary to

105

keep the paste from drying out while it's working.

It's not an easy job—you have to scrub well and you may have to rinse and rescrub a couple of times, but it will usually get the job done.

Paint thinner or engine degreaser may help to clean an old oil stain from a hard surface. First saturate the stain with thinner or degreaser, then use the kitty litter or corn starch treatment described above.

"Spots" on clothing are not "stains". Spots can become stains if they are not treated properly.

Avoid setting a fabric stain by ironing over it or placing the article of clothing in the dryer.

When attempting to remove stains, wet only as necessary to risk spreading the stain.

Work from the back of the fabric when removing stains to flush the stain back out rather than through the fabric.

Many fabrics recommend dry cleaning only. In such cases, pin a note to the stain identifying its origin if possible and always point it out to your dry cleaner.

Professional cleaners have their own chemicals and bag of tricks for removing stains. Most will be able to tell you what the chances are of eliminating the stain.

If the cleaner doesn't give you much hope for removing the stain, try the home remedy. Whatcha got to lose?

REMOVING SPOTS AND STAINS

To remove ball-point pen ink stains, cover thoroughly with hair spray and dab off with a clean, dry cloth.

Ball-point pen ink can often be removed with nail polish remover, but test first to be sure it is safe on the fabric. Place an absorbent towel over the ink stain and dab on nail polish remover from the opposite side of the fabric.

To remove rust from fabric, cover the stain with lemon juice and salt, then allow to dry in the sun. Repeat if necessary. Use enough lemon to wet the spot, then top with a liberal coating of salt.

For fabric such as carpeting that can't be taken up to lay in the sun, use a sun lamp. Position the bulb directly over the stain, at least three inches from the fabric. Monitor regularly to be sure that the fabric is not bein scorched. The treatment will take thirty to forty–five minutes.

Many fabric stains can be removed with a bar of white hand soap. After an initial flushing with water, rub on the soap; wash and rinse thoroughly.

Before working on a stain caused by wax, remove the wax itself. Scrape or peel wax from a hard surface; do not scrape or peel from a fabric as it may cause damage. Cover the wax with an absorbent paper towel and melt it off with a hot iron—the wax well be absorbed by the toweling. For a fabric, apply the toweling to both sides.

To remove grease and automotive oil from cotton clothing, rub shortening into the stain and then overlap with a paste of water and laundry detergent, rubbing it into the material. Wash as usual.

To restore color changed by ammonia, rinse the discolored area thoroughly with water, apply a few drops of white vinegar and rinse again with water.
For wool and silk, dilute the vinegar with an equal amount of water and test first to be sure the dye is colorfast.

To correct colors changed by vinegar, rinse with water and blot with a few drops of diluted ammonia on a cotton ball, then rinse with water again.

To remove chocolate, use a three percent solution of hydrogen peroxide. Peroxide is safe for all fabrics, but should be first tested to be sure the dye is colorfast.

White vinegar removes mustard, wax and jelly stains. Vinegar is safe for all fibers, but should be tested to be sure the dye is colorfast.

Vinegar stops the action of bleach! To reduce the damage of a spill, dab on vinegar with a cloth or sponge as quickly as possible.

REMOVING SPOTS AND STAINS

To remove most fruit juice stains, flush, then soak the garment in cold water. If necessary, apply a little detergent after the soaking and rinse thoroughly.

Stubborn fruit juice stains may be removed with peroxide after making sure it is safe on the garment.
Place an absorbent towel over the stain and drizzle peroxide from the opposite side. Blot up bubbles and repeat until bubbles stop forming.

To remove grass stains from fabric, rinse the garment in water, then dab the stain with alcohol and blot dry from both sides.

Grass stains may be removed with a mixture of one part vinegar to two parts water; dab on and blot dry from both sides.

Fresh wine stains may be removed from fabric by blotting up as much as possible from both sides, rinsing in club soda, then cold water.

Red wine spills can be neutralized by immediately covering the area with salt.

If red or blush wine stain persists, try blotting with a mixture of one part vinegar to two parts water; rinse and wash as usual.

Many fresh stains can be absorbed by corn starch or talcum powder. Simply sprinkle the powder over the stain, allow to stand for about an hour, then brush off carefully. Place a napkin or toweling under the stain to protect the tabletop, other materials, etc.

Waterless hand cleaner is an excellent spot remover, even for old stains. Find one at your grocery, hardware, or automotive store that has suggestions on the container for removing stains.

Avoiding Laundry Blues

Preparation

Check the pockets before you launder. Sounds too simple to even mention, but think about what a misplaced lipstick, book of matches, tissue, or (heaven forbid) a crayon can do to your load of wash.

Remove pins, buckles and any other object that can catch on clothing before laundering; close zippers and fasten hooks.

Separate the lint givers from the lint takers when you sort the laundry.
You quickly learn to identify those articles of clothing or linens that <u>always</u> seem to give off tons of lint and those that tend to attract the slightest bit.

❀

Garments that attract lint should be turned inside out to keep the outside from becoming coated with lint.

❀

Wash fragile garments inside out—the garment will suffer less from the action of the agitator.
Garments with silk screened designs and jeans profit especially from this treatment.

To avoid harming fabrics by direct contact with detergent, add it to the wash water and allow it to mix well before adding clothes.

Don't overcrowd the washer. Two small loads are better than one large one—the action of the washer will clean the clothes better.

Begin to add clothes after the agitation starts to be sure that they tumble freely for best cleaning and, most important, complete rinsing.

Always wash a new garment by itself. Seems wasteful, but you only have to do it once, and you may preserve the color of several other garments.

When washing colored fabric for the first time, add about one cup of vinegar per large load to cold wash water to set the dye and prevent future bleeding of colors.

Most garments wash well in warm or cold water and they will last longer.

Avoid washing garments with elastic in hot water. The heat will hasten destruction of the elasticity.

Resist the temptation to use extra soap. Extra soap is difficult to rinse out and may remain in the garments, which can dull colors and be irritating to the skin. At the very least it makes clothing stiff.

AVOIDING LAUNDRY BLUES

Sorting the laundry is a good idea, but... sometimes it's tough to make decisions. Try a Bachelor Sort: separate clothes to be bleached from those that absolutely cannot be bleached, then sort lights and darks.

If whites are not separated they will always pick up some color from other garments, even those that have been washed many times.

Always wash matching sets together in the same load: hold an odd sock until you find its mate; if you wash the top of a sweat suit, wash the bottom even if it is clean, otherwise the color may never again match.

Garments that are normally bleached can be added to an unbleached load, but NEVER add an non-bleach garment to a bleach load.

Wash the plastic shower curtain in the clothes washer with a couple of bath towels. The towels will tumble against the shower curtain and help to clean it. Hang the curtain up to dry.

When washing a plastic shower curtain retard the formation of mildew by adding ½ cup of table salt to the water and allowing the curtain to soak for fifteen minutes. Drain washer and remove the curtain—no need to spin.

Other Care Tips

Smooth wrinkled garments by placing them on hangers in the bathroom and running hot water in the shower for a few minutes with the bathroom door closed.

Those little hand steamers that appeared on the market a few years ago work well. Drape a thick towel over a door. Twist the neck of a clothes hanger so that it fits over the top of the door and allows the garment on it to press against the towel which will soak up condensation from the steam. Begin with seams; move the steamer slowly and pull lightly to keep seams straight as you go.

Remove fuzz balls from sweaters with a shaver. Go over the surface slowly and carefully with a disposable razor. If you can abide one more gadget, fabric shavers are inexpensive and effective.

To reshape a shrunken wool sweater, try soaking the garment in two tablespoons of hair cream rinse mixed with a gallon of cool water, then roll in a towel to remove excess water and clothespin to a pants stretcher or board. Stretch a bit by pulling seams gently but firmly at the shoulders, sides, and neck.

A zipper will slide easier if rubbed with soap or paraffin.

AVOIDING LAUNDRY BLUES

To keep tight jeans from getting tighter, keep them out of the dryer. It's that hot dry heat that does the dastardly deed. Spread them out to dry flat, or use two coated hangers—drape one pant leg over each and hang in the bathroom. For faster drying, drape them over two chairs near a heater or vent.

To sanitize bedding, remove the sheets from the bed carefully, folding them in toward the center in order to minimize spreading bacteria, etc. Wash them in the hottest water possible with detergent and borax.

To sanitize wash cloths and towels, wash them in hot water with detergent and allow them to dry in the sun.

To keep a fresh smell in the linen closet or drawer, leave a few used dryer sheets or an unwrapped bar of soap with the clothes.

Clean mineral deposits from a steam iron by filling it with a mixture of equal parts of distilled water and white vinegar. Allow it to steam for several minutes, then disconnect and let the iron stand for an hour. Empty the reservoir, rinse it well, refill with distilled water, and allow it to steam briefly to clear the vents.

To avoid the formation of mineral deposits in a steam iron, use distilled water only in the reservoir.
For free distilled water, catch rainwater in a non metal container.

HANDY HOUSEHOLD HINTS

To remove burned on starch from an iron place a towel dampened with vinegar on the ironing board and sprinkle it generously with table salt. Set the iron on warm dry setting and run over the towel until the stain is removed.

Clean gunk off the surface of an iron by polishing it gently with 0000 grade steel wool. Don't try this with a non-stick iron as the steel wool will remove the coating.

If an iron surface is dull, polish it with pearl drops or other tooth paste; it will slide easier and press better.

If you use a self–service laundry, keep a laundry kit that's always ready to go with a box of detergent, dryer sheets, etc. and a small bag for coins.

Between launderings, drop in change when you empty your pocket or purse.

If you don't want add to your burden by carrying a box of detergent, measure the amount required for each load into plastic bags. When you are ready to go, so are they.

Be sure to clean seasonal clothing that is to be stored. Not only do stains get tougher to remove over time, but they can attract unwanted pests.

Moths don't eat fabric; they damage it while eating food stains and the like that are in the fabric.

Save those used drier sheets. Put them over wire hangers to protect clothing and keep them smelling fresh.

Repairing & Refinishing

Before Calling a Professional

Find a good hardware store. That's a place staffed by professionals who know their business and are never too busy to explain things to you. Treat them well, take them out to lunch, bake cookies, whatever it takes—they are worth their weight in gold.

Many necessary repairs can be easily accomplished with correct answers to dumb questions asked by those of us who are not initiated into the inner workings of our home and appliances.

Don't wait for things to go wrong: locate all the shutoffs for electricity, gas, water, etc. so that you can find them quickly in an emergency.

Label fuses or circuit breakers in the main box so that you don't have to shut off everything if it's not necessary. For water, locate the main shutoff valve as well as those near sinks, toilets, dish and clothes washer, etc.

117

When you have a leaking water pipe, try to determine the source of the leak, that is, whether there is a hole in the pipe or a leaking joint.

PVC pipe can often be repaired with an epoxy compound available at most hardware stores. A metal fitting that unscrews can often be replaced. Just be sure to turn off the water before you remove the fitting and keep a bucket handy to catch any water left in the pipe.

To defrost frozen pipes, open the tap and begin heating with a hair dryer at the tap. As the ice melts, move on down the pipe. Take care not to overheat the pipe or it may burst and keep in mind that the hair dryer is hooked up to electricity—wear rubber soled shoes and avoid standing in any runoff water.

If you don't have a hair dryer, wrap the pipe in cloths that have been dipped in hot water.

A drop in the flow of water from a faucet may indicate only a blocked aerator. If you have one, it's a little doo-hickey with a fine–mesh screen in it screwed on at the end of the faucet.

Turn off the water, unscrew the piece at the end of the faucet, and flush out the screen, taking care not to drop it out of its fitting.

A leaky faucet shouldn't be ignored. Often a new washer is all you need to fix the problem, but if the leak is allowed to continue, escaping water will eventually eat away the washer seat requiring that the entire fixture be replaced. Most sinks have a water shutoff valve under them on the line leading up to the faucet.

If you aren't sure how the faucet comes apart, check your local hardware store for a similar model and get some tips from a member of the staff. Once you've taken the faucet apart you can return to the store with a sample of the washer and anything else you need to replace.

When the toilet tank runs all the time, it may only need adjustment. Remove the tank cover. If the mechanism is the type that has a ball about the size of a grapefruit at the end of a long rod, you may be able to rectify the problem easily.

The ball, or float, is normally pushed upward by the pressure of water in the tank forcing the other end downward to shut off the water. Gently lift the ball—if the water stops running, the shutoff is worn or coated with minerals and requires a bit more pressure to close completely. Carefully bend the rod slightly so that the float is pushed further downward into the water. Don't overdo it—bend the rod just a little at a time and test it. Correctly adjusted, the water will shut off just as the water in the tank reaches its normal level.

If a minor adjustment doesn't fix a running toilet, your local hardware store clerk can be of great assistance.

There are different systems, so you need to be able to identify one similar to yours in the store. The units aren't as complicated as they look and replacement parts are readily available in most cases.

Don't neglect drains that are partly constricted; correct the problem before it gets serious. For a slight clog, check first for hair or some other obstruction in the drain. What appears to be only a few strands of hair clinging to the cross pieces may well be supporting a large clump of hair underneath.

If that fails, try a plunger or pour about a quarter of a cup of baking soda down the drain followed by a quarter of a cup of vinegar. When the foaming stops, plug the opening and fill the sink with hot water; then pull the plug to release the full weight of the water against the clog.

If you use a plunger, fix it firmly against the drain and allow running water to rise up around it. Work it in short, rapid strokes to dislodge the obstruction.

Keep the plunger tight against the drain opening as you work to create and maintain a vacuum in the line to help dislodge the obstruction.

When the washer or dryer stops working, be sure the load is balanced; some machines stop automatically if the tub cannot turn freely.

Washers and dryers that stop when the lid is open have a small button that is depressed by the closed lid. Be sure that the lid is properly closed and that the button is not jammed.

A front loader that will not run may have a piece of a garment stuck in the door, preventing it from closing tightly.

A leaking clothes washer may be caused by a damaged or disconnected hose that is easily repaired or replaced.
Hoses wear out over time and connections can come loose, especially if the machine vibrates a lot. For a replacement, measure to determine the length you will need, then cut a section from the damaged hose to take to the hardware store with you to be sure that you get the right size and type of hose needed.

A washer may appear to be leaking when it is simply overloaded. Make sure that's not the cause of water on the floor before you go to a lot of trouble.

When the dryer does not dry or takes too long to dry, the air flow may be restricted. Check the lint trap, and be sure that the outside vent is not clogged.

Even an apparently clean lint trap may harbor a fine coat of oily dust that restricts air flow. Periodically scrub the screen with water and a liquid detergent, then rinse it well and wipe it dry.

Electrical problems are best left to experts, but there are some simple problems you can solve.

When an appliance fails to work, for example, check the fuse box or circuit breaker, then try it in another outlet to determine whether the appliance or the electrical circuit is at fault.

A fuse or circuit breaker that blows regularly may indicate an overload. Check to see what you have on that circuit—many appliances pull a lot of current when they start up and your problem may be that two of them on the same circuit often start up at the same time.

Unless you want to face the cost of rewiring, your only recourse is to plug them into different circuits.

Never use a fuse larger than that specified on the circuit—you face the risk of fire!

If problems persist, it's time to call an electrician.

Replacing a broken pane of glass is quite simple.

First, wearing sturdy gloves, chip off the putty with a putty knife. Take out the remaining glass and the glazier's points, those little metal triangles that hold the glass in place. Notice where the glazier's points are—you don't need to replace them exactly, but it will give you a good idea of how it's done.

The hardware store or glass shop will cut the pane to size for you; when you measure, be sure to allow for overhang in the frame and bring along a sample of the glass to be sure you get the correct thickness. Replace the glass, tap in the glazier's points, and finally, the putty. Allow the putty to set before painting.

If you don't have glazier's points, or if you are afraid of breaking the glass, simply apply small spots of household cement to hold the glass while you putty.

Color window putty to match surrounding trim by mixing a bit of paint with the putty before applying.
Be sure to use a paint that matches the putty—that is, if the putty is water–based, the paint should be as well.

To remove a broken bulb from a light fixture, make certain the power is off and use a pair of long–nosed pliers to remove as much of the glass as possible. With one hand on each handle of the pliers, insert them into the base of the bulb and open the pliers so that the press against the sides, then turn carefully.

We've also seen bulbs removed with a potato! After making certain that the power is off, trim the end of the potato to fit into the fixture and jam it into the remaining glass around the edge of the bulb. Turn gently, and the bulb should come out.

Working with Plaster and Drywall

Before patching a large hole, fashion a backing of wire mesh to give the new plaster something to cling to. Nudge the mesh into the hole and secure it to beams or lathing with small nails or staples.

The mesh should be large enough to allow some of the plaster to fit through the holes, but small enough that large gobs won't go through and fall off in back, defeating its purpose. Check the hardware store for material designed for just such a project.

Large cracks in plaster can be stuffed with steel wool or newspaper to fill them somewhat before applying new plaster.

To repair a large hole in drywall use a piece of drywall cut to size and held in with *drywall repair clips* available at most hardware stores or lumber yards.

Plaster can also be used to patch holes or large cracks in drywall. Proceed as outlined above for plaster walls.

Fill large holes in two or three stages. Apply plaster filler in several thin coats rather than one thick one for better drying and less shrinkage. Leave the surface rough on all but the last coat.

Smooth off plaster or drywall repairs with a thin spackling compound.

If you are not an experienced spackler, do the best you can, then smooth with a fine sandpaper and use a thin coat of spackle to fill imperfections.

To match the color of the wall after patching, find a paint or hardware store that has a computer matching system. They can duplicate almost any color.

To fill tiny holes in plaster or drywall, such as from a nail or picture hook when you don't have any putty or spackling compound, use toothpaste. Simply dab some in the hole with your fingers.

Before driving a nail into plaster, cover the spot with transparent tape to hold the plaster together, then drill a pilot hole.

Small pictures can be hung from drywall using hooks designed for the purpose or with a nail driven in at a 45° angle.

To hang heavy objects from plaster or drywall, use screws and anchors. A variety of anchors designed for that purpose are available at the hardware store. Take along a sample of the drywall if you're not sure of the thickness.

To keep pictures on the wall straight, wrap adhesive or masking tape around the center of the wire to keep it from slipping in the hanger.

A larger picture may require two hooks, both to carry the weight and to insure that it remains straight.
You may want to use two hooks on a smaller picture that doesn't want to hang straight.

Working with Wood

A loose table or chair leg that screws in may be tightened by wrapping the threads with cotton cord.

Avoid using glue to repair a leg that screws in. If the hole is already enlarged or somehow damaged, the glue probably won't hold up when the chair is put back into service and you have the additional problem of dealing with the glue when you try to repair it again.

Most glues will not adhere well to previously glued wood. The original coat of glue will have penetrated and sealed the wood and a new coating will not adhere well to the old glue or the wood.

To reattach previously glued surfaces, remove all of the old adhesive, cut ridges into both surfaces, apply fresh glue to the pieces, and reattach them. Pack any space around the joint with shims made from wood slivers.

To tighten a leg or rung that has been previously glued, cut a slit in the center of the piece and drive in a thin wedge to spread it. Take care not to spread the piece so far that it cracks.

Make a paste of white glue and sawdust to pack a leg or rung that is loose.

To improve the action of sticking drawers, rub soap or wax on the runners.

Sticking drawers can be caused by swelling from moisture. Take out the drawer and dry the wood with a hair dryer, then coat with a good wood sealer.

To tighten a loose screw when the hole has become too large, pack the hole with a wooden match, a toothpick, or a splinter of wood.

To tighten a screw when the hole is only slightly oversized, wrap a little steel wool around the screw or dip the screw in wood glue.

Screws and nails drive easier if they are first rubbed over a bar of soap.

Before driving small nails, tap the sharp end lightly with a hammer. Slightly flattening the end will keep it from splitting delicate molding.

To save your fingers when driving small nails, use a narrow strip of cardboard, synthetic sponge, or a thin scouring pad to hold the nail.

To replace very small screws, dip the end of the screwdriver in glue so that the screw will stick to the screwdriver.

REPAIRING AND REFINISHING

When working in tight spaces, push the screw through the gummed side of a piece of masking tape. Then insert the screwdriver in the screw slot and pull the tape back to attach the screw firmly to the driver.

For a better grip on a screw head, dip the screwdriver tip into baking soda or an abrasive cleaner.

To drill a large hole accurately, first drill a small pilot hole.

To make sanding easier, moisten the back of the sandpaper and wrap it around a block of wood.

Before sanding soft wood, apply a thin coat of shellac and allow to dry. The wood will sand much smoother.

For a super–smooth finish, use 0000 grade steel wool for the final sanding.

Remove scratches from hardwood floors with 0000 grade steel wool dipped in paste wax. Be sure to rub in the direction of the grain

When reassembling furniture, if a hammer is necessary to drive two pieces together, be sure to cushion the blows to prevent marking. Do so by placing a bit of scrap wood over the piece you are striking or put a large adhesive bandage over the face of the hammer.

Painting

A fresh coat of paint is the easiest way to give furniture or a room a crisp, new look

Before painting, taking the time to clean and prepare the surface well will pay big dividends in the finished job.
Sand or patch blemishes, fill holes, etc. that mar the surface. Thoroughly brush the walls or furniture to be painted in order to get rid of loose dirt, then wash with water mixed with a small amount of a light detergent.
Extremely smooth painted or varnished surfaces need to be roughened so that the new paint will stick. You can sand them, but it's much easier to use a product called *liquid sandpaper*—you just brush it on like a primer coat.

Invest in good quality paint. The few extra dollars is worth it when the paint goes on easier and requires only one coat instead of two, or two coats instead of three or four.

130

When you are painting only to change the look of a room, and you already have a good base coat, you may want to sponge on a complementary color. For an interesting texture, use a good sea sponge. Take care not to get too much paint on the sponge—keep lots of newspapers around to dab off any excess.

If you have never tried anything like this before, you may want to experiment first in a small area that will be easy to paint over or using a piece of scrap lumber. (And, as the effect is heightened by showthrough, you might be just as happy with an inexpensive paint.)

Good brushes may be a smart investment as well. A good brush makes the job easier and if properly cleaned will last a lifetime. If you do opt for an inexpensive brush that you can throw away after the job is done, watch out for stray hairs that can wind up on the surface as you paint.

If you use a paint roller, be sure to get one suited to the surface you are painting.

A smooth surface generally calls for a roller with short fibers; to achieve a textured look or for a rough surface, use a thick or fluffy roller.

Line a roller tray with plastic or aluminum foil to simplify cleanup.

Instead of a roller tray, take a tip from the professionals— pour the paint into a bucket wide enough to accommodate the full width of the roller and hang a roller screen, available at most paint stores, inside the bucket. When you dip the roller into the paint and run it over the screen, the paint is more evenly distributed and the excess paint flows back into the bucket.

Cut down the time you spend on a ladder. You may have to get close to the edge where the ceiling meets the wall in order to cut a fine line with a paint brush or pad, but once that is done, use a long–handled roller to do the rest of the job from a comfortable position on the floor. Buy a roller with a hollow, threaded handle that will accommodate a broom or mop handle.

Use water–based paint whenever possible, as cleanup is much easier and more environmentally friendly.

Wrap brushes carefully in water–soaked newspaper when you take a break from painting with water–based paint; a few strokes on dry newspaper will get rid of the excess water on the brush when you're ready to start again.

When you have a paint job that takes more than one day, wrap brushes or rollers in film wrap or a plastic bag and place in the refrigerator overnight. Just take them out the next day, allow them to warm up and you're ready to go.

Hate to clean brushes? Consider inexpensive brushes or pads and throw them away when you are done.

Place strips of wet newspaper over the carpet or floor where it meets a wall you are painting, The wet paper will stick to the baseboard and remain in place to soak up any drips.
Use a spray bottle of water to wet the papers.

Protect the rest of the floor with a good drop cloth. A heavy drop cloth is not very expensive, and will relieve you of the irritation caused by dry newspapers or light plastic slipping out of place or sticking to your shoes!

To protect against paint spatters, cover hardware on furniture and surrounding trim on walls with a thin coat of petroleum jelly which can be wiped off after painting.
Works well on hands and face too; rub on the petroleum jelly much as you would sun tan lotion. When the job is done, the jelly washes off easily with soap and water taking paint spots with it.
Doesn't hurt to rub some in your hair as well when painting a ceiling—it also washes out easily.

Protect your fingernails before working with paint by scratching a bar of soap to force a protective layer of the soap under them.

Remove oil base paint from hands and face with baby oil instead of turpentine.

To protect glass when painting windows, cover the glass with strips of wet newspaper.

To clean paint or excess putty from window panes, soften first with turpentine and scrape off with a razor knife or sharpened putty knife.

To protect stored paint, cut a circle the size of the paint can top out of aluminum foil or wax paper and place directly on the surface of the paint in the can. This will prevent a crust from forming on the top and keep the paint clean.

Left over oil base paint can be protected by adding a thin layer of mineral spirits to the top of the paint in the can; simply mix it in the next time you use the paint.

Paint can also be stored with the cans upside down to keep extra air from leeching into the can and to make mixing easier for the next use.

A professional painter once suggested leaving the can open to allow a skin to form on the top of the paint before closing the can. The next time the paint is to be used, remove the skin and, if necessary, add a little water or mineral spirits depending on the type of paint.

With this method, dirt or rust from the lid doesn't get mixed into the paint.

Save wide–mouthed jars for cleaning paint brushes. The cleaner can be left in the jar, tightly closed; within a few days the paint will settle to the bottom and the clean thinner can be poured off for re-use. A coffee can may be used, but it will rust if allowed to sit for very long.

Make your ladder safe by wrapping burlap around the bottom rung to wipe your feet before climbing.

In addition, when you back down the ladder you know when you are on the last rung!

For easier pouring from a paint can, cover the recess around the top of the can with tape. Pouring is neater, and when the tape is removed, the rim is clean to insure a tight seal.

To catch drips from the side of a paint can, glue a paper plate to the bottom of the can.

You can also punch holes around the rim of the can to allow any paint that collects to drain back into the can. This not only saves paint and keeps the rim clean, but helps to avoid drips as well.

After removing hardware from an area to be painted insert pipe cleaners in the screw holes to keep from filling them with paint.

Before painting over a water stain, use a portable hair dryer to be sure the area is completely dry, then seal with a coat of shellac. Sealing the stain will reduce the chance that it will bleed through the paint.

When painting stairs, paint every other step one day, the remaining steps another day. That way you won't be confined to one part of the house while the paint dries.

To paint a door, remove it first! Most heavy hinges have a center pin that allows easy removal. With the door off its hinges, you will be sure to cover all of the edges thoroughly and evenly. The top and bottom edges are the most likely places for moisture to seep in and create expansion that can in turn cause the door to stick.

If the door is paneled, laying it flat for painting will avoid those nasty drips that sneak in on your work.

Create a textured look on a single piece of furniture or a wall. The technique involves applying a solid base coat with a roller or brush, then dabbing on one or more additional harmonious colors with a sponge, a cloth, or crumpled plastic wrap. Some tips:

• The sponge needs to be large, preferably natural, with large holes to create a varying pattern. If cloth or plastic wrap is used they should be only crumpled lightly, also to achieve an interesting pattern. When the applicator gets too full of paint or won't hold its shape, wash it out or replace it.

• Begin the texturing by using very little paint. Pat the applicator on newspapers to get rid of excess if necessary. Cover an area large enough to envision the effect, turning the applicator as you go in order to vary the pattern. If a color needs to be more prominent, you can always go back over the area again.

• Colors are applied one at a time, but additional shades can be applied over a wet texture coat. Just be sure the application is light enough to keep it all from blending into a single color. You will probably get different effects from applying over wet versus dry, so keep the technique the same for uniform results.

• This is a unique work of art, so don't rush it.

• And here's a plus—if you don't like the results you can paint over it and start again.

The colors may be dark on light or light on dark. We read of one project that involved using five shades of gray to emulate the look of marble. Usually the treatment is applied to only one wall of a room, but it can work for an entire room.

We've not tried this, only seen others do it. It looks like fun and we're going to try it, but we plan to practice on old boards first. You may want to do the same.

We did paint a small wood building to look like barn siding. We applied a dark tone over a lighter base coat that had not completely dried using an old stiff brush. We made thin vertical lines with the very tips of the bristles that had been just barely dipped into the paint, then pressed the brush hard against the wall at varying intervals and twisted it to emulate knots and other faux imperfections.

Think twice about painting over stained or mildewed surfaces. The stain will bleed through the paint in no time. Usually, cleaning the surface well and shellacking over the stain will do the job, but we have seen one instance where a stain persisted through several coats of shellac. In that case, the owner opted to live with it considering that the only alternative we could suggest was to knock out the panel and replace it.

Refinishing Furniture

Before you shop at an antique or unfinished furniture store, check out garage sales, your local Salvation Army, or Goodwill outlet. Your reward could be a fine piece of furniture that needs only a new finish ...and at a reasonable price!

The suggestions for restoring a finish that follow can apply to all types of furniture; just be sure to test first in an in-

conspicuous place so as to avoid marring an old finish or
creating a new one you don't like.

A mild solution of detergent and water may be all you
need to restore the finish of an old piece of furniture.
It could take several washings, but don't try to hurry the
process with abrasive cleaners or a scouring pad—you
could scratch an original finish that is worth saving.

You can often recover the shine on the finish of an old
piece of furniture by wiping down with a soft cloth
dampened with alcohol.

Cleaning with alcohol may be best for furniture that carries
the burden of generations of greasy dirt and wax. Just
dampen a rag and rub. The alcohol won't harm an original finish of paint or lacquer.
The alcohol will attack shellac, but once cleaned thoroughly, you can easily apply a fresh coat.

Oil soap is an excellent cleaner for surfaces that are lightly
soiled. Once the oil soap has dried, you can use a dry,
soft cloth to buff to a nice sheen.

**To remove the old finish from small grooves in turned
legs** after you have applied a paint remover, use a piece

of cotton string or yarn. Hold the string taut and run it back and forth in the groove as you work your way around the leg.

To remove paint remover or cleaner from grooves in a decorative surface, sharpen the end of a small dowel with a knife or pencil sharpener and use it to poke into slots and grooves. You thus eliminate the chance of damage that a metal tool can create.

A small, stiff, artist's brush may be adequate for cleaning intricate work. Keep a cloth handy to wipe the brush clean as you work.

Before you take a piece of furniture completely apart to refinish it or reglue the joints, mark each of the pieces that fit together with masking tab. Use a letter or number system so that A goes with A, B with B, etc. to be sure that everything goes back the way it was.

Variations in the slats from the back of a chair or in the legs of a table, created when the piece was first built or imposed by wear, may be subtle, but they can be a huge problem if you try to put them back together incorrectly.

Before painting furniture, decide on the look you want. Water–based paint is easiest to use and it is available in a variety of finishes from flat to high gloss or wet look enamel. Each type of finish has a unique charm; try to

picture how the piece will look with the finish you prefer, and how it will look alongside other pieces of furniture that you plan to have in the same area.

Consider dressing up furniture with decoupage. It's not
too difficult, but we recommend practice before decorating a treasured piece.
- Find the print you want to use—a design from wallpaper, a picture from a magazine, a photo, or even a
  piece of fabric. Rough cut the design first, then carefully trim with sharp scissors, keeping in mind that the
  edge doesn't have to be perfect.
- Decoupage requires a very smooth, preferably fresh—
  painted, surface. If not freshly painted, rub down lightly
  with 0000 grade steel wool to be sure that it is absolutely smooth.
- On the back of the print, brush a very thin coat of decoupage finish, available at most handicraft stores.
  Place the print where you want it to go and pat over the
  entire surface with a damp sponge, working from the
  center to the outer edges to eliminate any air bubbles
  and excess coating.
- Once the print is dry, a matter of a few minutes, brush
  on two coats of decoupage finish, allowing about thirty
  minutes drying time between coats.

Polish with toothpaste! Clean and polish high gloss surfaces by rubbing with toothpaste, letting it dry and then
buffing to a nice shine.

Rubbing in the direction of the grain is always most effective when cleaning or refinishing wood furniture.

Use an old toothbrush for cleaning or staining intricate scrollwork on furniture and picture frames. First, clean the brush by soaking in a glass of water containing a teaspoonful of bleach.

Soiled or spotted marble tops can be cleaned by covering with a folded paper towel that has been wet with full strength hydrogen peroxide. Cover the towel with a sheet of plastic wrap, weigh down with a book or other heavy object, and check in an hour or two. If the stain is not gone, continue the process.

When staining raw wood, rub it down first with alcohol to bring out the grain.

Use a rag to apply stain and rub it in as you go to avoid over–darkening. Reapply the stain to add additional color if necessary.
This method also makes it easy to adjust the base color as well by mixing stains or using an entirely different stain for the second coat.

Quick touchup stain can be made from instant coffee dissolved in a small amount of water.

Strong brewed tea makes a good antique stain.

Make a stain from coffee grounds. Allow the wet grounds to stand for a few days in a closed container, then squeeze out the liquid for a fine touchup stain.

Stain new wood with a food or cloth dye. You can achieve some interesting effects with a weak solution of red green or blue. Test first in an inconspicuous place and opt for a light tone as different wood will create dissimilar results and the color may darken as it dries—you can always darken later if you want to.

And be sure to wear rubber or plastic gloves unless you want to dye your hands as well.

Other fascinating results can be obtained by combining a dye with a stain or overcoating a dye with a stain. This technique calls for lots of testing on scrap lumber first, then in an inconspicuous place on the piece being refinished, but the outcome can be most gratifying.

Before staining or painting, use a tack cloth (available at most hardware or paint stores) to wipe away any fine particles of dust or other residue.

For a smooth stained finish, rub down with 0000 grade steel wool between coats.

When applying stain, cover your hands with a small plastic bag that can be discarded when the job is complete.

Scratches on light finished furniture can be hidden by using tan shoe polish.

To repair fine scratches on furniture cover with petroleum jelly overnight. Rub in well, remove excess and buff.

To cover scratches on wood furniture, rub a matching color crayon into the scratch and smooth with the fingers. Heat and oil from your finger will blend in the crayon.

Use cigarette ashes or damp tea leaves to shade an application and create a look of aging.

To fix light scratches or blemishes on walnut, rub the scratch with a piece of walnut or pecan meat, then wax with the product you normally use.

For mahogany, rub the scratch with a dark brown crayon or a brown commercial wax product, then buff with your fingers, then a cloth.

To fix a scratch on red mahogany, apply ordinary iodine with a small brush and wax with the product you normally use.

For maple, add iodine to denatured alcohol to get the right color and apply with a Q–tip, then dry, wax and buff.

To restore ebony, use black shoe polish, black eyebrow pencil, or black crayon.

For teakwood, rub very gently with 0000 steel wool. Rub in equal amounts of linseed oil and turpentine.

Other Tips and Fixes

Hang a small peg board in a closet or laundry room to keep a few tools handy in the house.

Use a bucket or tool carrier to keep a few basic tools handy when you need them and to save steps by carrying the necessary tools to do a specific job.

Wrap the handle of tools with adhesive or electrician's tape to insure a firm and safe grip.

Tape a piece of foam or rubber to a wooden hammer handle to absorb some of the shock when hammering.

Tape foam to the pressure point on shears or tin snips to keep from blistering your hands.

Before removing a sticking door to plane it down, check the hinges and trim. Often the problem is caused by a door that is sagging on a loose hinge or catching on loose molding.

To fix a door that swells and sticks in damp weather, dry out the area that has swelled with a hair dryer and then apply a sealer to keep out additional moisture.

To relieve sticking windows, try rubbing soap or candle wax in the channel.

Windows that stick due to swelling from moisture may be dried out with a hair dryer, but the fix will be temporary unless the wood can be sealed.

If you can remove the sticking window, dry the wood well with a hair dryer and then shellac to seal.

To prevent rust on tools cover them with a paste wax.

Use moth balls to soak up moisture in a tool box and prevent rust. Those little silica packs that are packaged with some products can be effective as well.

To repair a small hole in a screen, use clear nail polish or a clear household cement.

Protect hands from steel wool slivers by making a holder from half a rubber ball.

For a stronger bond when gluing furniture, add a few fibers of steel wool to the glue.

When you need heavy duty soap, try pre–wash laundry spray to clean your hands.

Lubricate door hinges with petroleum jelly instead of oil to prevent drips on the carpet.

Broken bathroom or kitchen tiles are almost impossible to match, so don't even try; use a contrasting color or painted tile for replacement. And they don't need to be in a regular pattern; a few contrasting tiles randomly placed can add a decorate touch.

Replace a broken toilet tank lid with a wooden one. Make the top from a piece of board or purchase a finished shelf from the hardware store.

You can size and finish it with a gloss paint in an attempt to make it look like the old cover, but unfortunately it will always look like an attempt. Better to make it larger than the tank top and paint or stain it to look like a shelf designed to fit over the tank

For a varnished surface damaged by ammonia, try applying a thin coat of liquid floor wax to restore the shine and texture. If the first coat is uneven because the wax is soaking in, reapply. If necessary, apply several light coats; don't try to apply a single heavy coat.

A varnished surface roughened by ammonia may be smoothed somewhat with 0000 grade steel wool, but be careful to lightly hit the high spots only: you don't want to cut through the varnish.

All Around the House

You don't need expensive and destructive chemicals to get rid of ant hills. Just sprinkle the ant hill with uncooked grits—the ants will feast for the last time.

Another remedy is to spread a layer of powdered cleanser over the hill and allow it to remain for two to three days. If it rains before three days pass, reapply.

Shun those chemical sprays for roaches. Just dust boric acid over the areas where you expect to find roaches or on any you see. The powder doesn't kill them immediately; it allows the creature to return to its nest and share the poison.

Candles burn better if they are frozen! Leave them in the freezer for an hour or two before lighting them and they will burn more slowly and evenly.

Use the coffee grounds to feed azaleas, or mix them in the garden soil or compost heap.

149

Roach proof your kitchen with a treatment of boric acid that can be purchased in any pharmacy. Use a squeeze bottle, bulb baster, or a container with holes in the lid to sprinkle the powder over cracks and crevices in pantry shelves, in kitchen and bathroom drawers, around major appliances, under sinks and around baseboards.

It may take a few days before the treatment will make a difference, but once it takes hold, the creatures disappear completely. For a more limited application, as around food, mix the boric acid with sugar, jelly or catsup and place in a bottle cap.

It is necessary to repeat the treatment only once or twice a year unless there is evidence of new activity, in which case apply to the area as necessary.

Roach proof your bathroom in the same fashion. Use a more specific application in the medicine chest and storage drawers.

To keep stray animals from the garbage sprinkle household ammonia over garbage bags and garbage can lids. Keep a spray bottle, clearly marked, for that purpose.

Be sure to respray after a rain and each time you put out the garbage

Generally, animals stick to their own territory and go only where they can find food. After a few non–productive visits you may find that you are no longer a part of the dinner tour, at least until other sources dry up or a new animal takes over the territory.

To repair a burn in a pile carpet, gather nap from a carpet scrap and shape into a ball the size of the burn. Attach the patch to the burned spot with clear household cement. Cover with a piece of smooth board and place a weight on top to allow the glue to set.

Hairline cracks in china can be repaired, or at least concealed, by simmering the dish in sweet milk over low heat for at least an hour.
Probably shouldn't trust those repaired dishes for serving food, but only for display.

Seal the end of nylon cord or rope by shellacking it or fusing it with the heat from a match or candle.

To lubricate a lock, rub the key with a very soft pencil and then turn the key in the lock several times. The graphite from the pencil is an excellent lubricant.
You could purchase a spray can of graphite lubricant, but you'll never use it all and it just takes up space.

To revive a counter top worn by time and cleaners try applying a thin coat of liquid floor wax.

To get rid of plants in the cracks of a sidewalk or patio sprinkle them with salt. Also effective for getting rid of unwanted pests such as poison ivy and snails

Increase shoe storage space with plastic milk crates laid on their side in the bottom of the closet. Use the half size crates to make the best use of space.

Those shoe bags that hang in the closet or on the closet door are great for storing odds and ends as well.

To remove the residue left by price stickers or labels, wipe them with mineral oil, vegetable oil, or peanut butter. Then wash with soap and water.

Fix a sink stopper that allows water to drain out by placing a piece of plastic wrap over the drain before inserting the stopper.

Need something to do in the winter? Get ready for summer. Look over the yard tools and see what kind of shape they're in. Scrape off rust with a wire brush and apply a coat of oil to prevent rust from reforming, replace split handles, and sharpen or send out for sharpening, any tools that need it.
This might be a good time to see if any equipment needs to be replaced. That will give you time to look for sales instead of paying top dollar at the height of the season.

Check gutters and downspouts regularly to be sure that they are secure and clear of debris that can cause a backup and possible damage to the roof. If you live in a wooded area, you may want to consider screens for the downspouts to keep them from becoming clogged with leaves.

Trim away branches that overhang the roof and could pose a problem in the future. The best time to trim is in the fall or spring.

Decorating

Don't overdo it. Granted, we're talking modest projects here, but just in case they inspire you to greater deeds, you may want to consider the advice of professionals who recommend that you don't undertake extensive re-modeling, inside or out, that can price your home out of its neighborhood if you decide to sell.

Personally, we consider changes in terms of the pleasure they will bring us, not what we can sell them for. There may be another consideration, however—if there is a chance you might want to sell in the near future, you should avoid any decorative touches that could turn off a prospective buyer and concentrate on those that have broader appeal such as a fresh coat of paint.

Have it your way! These are just ideas and concepts; often they're someone else's rules. You need to decide what it is that you like. If you want a room to appear small and intimate, ignore the ideas for making it look larger.

Build space around your needs and your lifestyle; whether its a place for pursuing a hobby, kicking back and relaxing, or entertaining friends, make it convenient and pleasant for you.

DECORATING

Look at your home as though you were seeing it for the first time. Take special note of small imperfections, and eliminate them first—a loose curtain rod, a crack in the wall, a stain on the ceiling.

A hallway is often ignored because we don't think of it as a room, but lots can be done to make a hallway interesting and even exciting:
- **Make it into an art gallery.** Line the walls, or even cover them, with your favorite artwork, posters, or craft projects. Here's an opportunity to display the things you like that don't quite fit into the decor of any other room.
- **Experiment with new techniques,** such as stenciling designs along woodwork or creating a textured look with a sponge on paint.
- **A narrow table or a small wall shelf for bric–a–brac** can break up the monotony of a long flat wall if the hall is wide enough to accommodate them.

Entryways also often receive too little attention. Hang an ornate mirror, a picture, or a wall sconce that will immediately attract the eye and create a homey feeling for anyone who enters. One of those old wrought iron garden seats would go well here.

Take a look outside as well...
- Think about what a visitor would notice first—spruce up the front yard and entryway.
- Clean up the patio and dress up the furniture with a

155

fresh coat of paint.

- Create a 'quiet place' out–of–doors. Set up a small plot for flowers, then add a bench or a couple of chairs nearby. Check out local garage sales and flea markets for old wrought iron garden seats.
- Consider an awning for a window that captures too much sunlight. A small one may do the job and be decorative from the outside as well.

Brighten up the outdoors with birds. Plants and bird feeders can attract a variety of colorful visitors. Find someone at a local garden center or contact your state wildlife office for information about which plants and feeders work in your area. A garden or bird feeder that can be viewed from a window will enhance indoor living as well.

A word of caution—some birds may come to rely on you for food, even to the point of not migrating as long as the weather is not too harsh, so don't slack off on putting food in the feeder year round.

Begin a new decorating project by deciding what you want to accomplish—a complete new look or sprucing up with a few touches here and there.

As you reflect on options, consider your lifestyle as well as fashion—such things as ease of upkeep or suitability for entertaining.

For a large project, set short and long term goals to keep the undertaking manageable and affordable.

DECORATING

Consider a color change carefully: the color of walls, ceilings, drapes or curtains, and carpets together will make a room dark or bright and change the appearance of the furniture in the room.

Neutral colors make a room seem larger, especially if carried throughout the room including in the carpeting and furnishings.

Painting the trim a contrasting color will add variety to a room.

Carry trim colors through the doorway from an adjoining room to achieve an interesting effect in a large room.

Painting one wall a different color or papering only one wall can create a dramatic effect.

Painting a small area can be dramatic as well. For instance, you can often change the look of the front of a house completely just by painting the front door, the door frame, or the columns and trim of a porch in a color that contrasts or complements that of the rest of the siding and trim.

Paint is not limited to plain colors. Interesting effects can be created with textured or variegated color paint kits available from most home improvement centers.

HANDY HOUSEHOLD HINTS

Wallpaper with vertical stripes will often make a ceiling seem higher.
Painting the ceiling a light color will add to the effect.

To make a ceiling seem lower, use wallpaper with a horizontal pattern or break the vertical line of the walls with trim such as a chair rail.

When wallpapering a small room, select a pattern that is small and light. Use bold or darker patterns only in larger rooms.

Rearrange the furniture! Change the feel of a room with a change in the visual effect. And don't overlook the possibility of moving furniture from one room to another.

It's easiest to rearrange furniture on a scale drawing of a room with templates cut from thick paper to represent the furniture. Be sure to consider the position of doors and windows, as well as additional space required, as for chairs around a table.

Furniture affects the perceived size of a room. Several tall pieces make the ceiling seem lower, bulky pieces make a room seem smaller, etc.

DECORATING

Don't hesitate to mix furniture styles. A mixture of styles, properly planned and placed, can serve to compliment each other.

Often you can tie different pieces together with accent elements, such as by color.

An unusual piece of furniture can create a focal point for a room, such as an ornate antique desk in a room full of modern furniture.

Before you buy new furniture, take a fresh look at what you have. You may find more to like than you realize:

- Light wood cupboards, tables, or chairs can often be stained darker and rubbed with oil for a deep rich look, or painted to bring color into a room.
- Dark wood can often be bleached and oiled for a lighter look.
- Change the look of furniture or cupboards by installing new hardware—hinges, drawer pulls, and handles.
- Throw pillows in a contrasting color or design can change the look of an otherwise serviceable sofa or easy chair.

Look around for ideas; be creative!

An aquarium can serve as an attractive and interesting focal point for a room.

Consider the affect of wall hangings. A large picture or hanging rug can dominate a room.

Sometimes a small touch such as a picture or a vase is all that is needed to make a part of the room perfect.

A group of small pictures can create an interesting focal point.

A few small pictures strategically placed, can break up the monotony of bare walls.
- Search through magazines and old books for prints to frame. Used book stores are a good source for prints as well as books of artwork.
- Give the pictures you have a new look with a new frame.

When hanging a picture, clock, etc. on a papered wall, cut an inverted V where you intend to place the nail or anchor, wet the area and carefully lift the paper flap so that the hole can be made in the wall only. When you remove the hanger, repaste the flap and hide the hole.

To keep pictures on the wall straight, wrap adhesive or masking tape around the center of the wire to keep it from slipping on the hanger.

A wall hanging over a piece of low furniture can help tie it in with surrounding taller furniture.

DECORATING

Oil paintings should not be matted or covered with glass; watercolors and prints may be matted and protected by glass if it makes them more attractive.

Make a room appear larger by hanging a mirror or mirrors on the wall.

An inexpensive window treatment can often alter the look of a room. Begin by considering what you want to achieve—privacy, more light, a window that looks larger, etc., and keep those things in mind as you look around for ideas. Here are a few thoughts:

- Make an 'ordinary' window look special by topping it with a prominent molding as described below.
- Flat or decorative molding surrounding a window, also described below, will make the window appear larger.
- Extending curtain rods and the curtains or drapes beyond the edge of a window will make it appear larger and more prominent.
- Let in lots of light by draping material over a bar at the top of the window (called a 'swag') instead of covering the window with a curtain. For a distinctive look, use decorative hangers embellished with ornate brightwork. You can make the room even brighter by using a colorful print for the swag.

When you shop for carpets or drapes, keep it simple—not the pattern, just the buying. Find the best quality in your price range, then look for something you like. If you shop

161

every fabric or carpet store looking for just the right pattern, you may never be able to make a decision among
the (literally) hundreds of samples available for you to
choose from. Same goes for wallpaper.

Make a door more prominent or a window appear larger
by adding molding around or over it. Begin by mounting
flat molding around the existing frame, then build it up
with combinations of other molding to create the effect
you want. Once the new molding is installed and all of
the edges have been sealed, paint the new and old molding with the same color to create the impression that it is
a single piece.

Visit your local hardware emporium or lumber yard to
get familiar with the various types of molding available
and for ideas. Many home repair centers have samples of
combination molding on display. Once you know what
is available, you will also understand how other elabo-
rate moldings were created from combinations.

Molding along the wall and ceiling joint will add a decorative touch to a room. We're not talking quarter round
here, but decorative molding. Check out your home center to see what's available. The toughest part is cutting
the mitered joints at the corners, but with a little care and
practice, the art can be mastered.

Create dramatic affects with lighting. Use track lighting
spots to highlight special elements in a room.

Indirect lighting softens colors and lines to create a warm, cozy atmosphere.

Fluorescent lighting brightens a room. Most hardware stores sell devices for converting incandescent fixtures to fluorescent.

For an interesting effect, paper a den or work room with road maps or posters. Cover with shellac to protect them; a weak solution of orange shellac creates an aged look.

Decorate a small section of wall or cupboard doors in the kitchen with wine labels. Merely glue them on like wallpaper and shellac over them.

To make a plain door more attractive, create a frame of decorative molding.

To decorate and protect the base of a door, make a panel of tiles or parquet flooring squares.

Use throw rugs in doorways and entries for added color, and to save wear and cleaning of heavily trafficked carpeted areas.

Brighten the tape and pulls on venetian blinds with white shoe polish.

Hanging drapes is easier if you stick the hooks in a bar of soap before inserting into the fabric.

Add simple touches with craft projects:
- Fill a glass vase, a large goblet, or a brandy snifter with small Christmas tree balls to set on a shelf or mantle any time of the year.
- Craft stores usually carry wooden cutouts of toys and such that you can paint or stain and glue to the corner of a picture frame or on a cupboard door.
- If the cutout is made from a soft wood, try staining with a food dye. (Be sure to protect your hands so that you don't stain them as well.)
- Or how about a toy train colored with a natural wood stain running along the top of a door frame?
- Make your own cutouts using templates of your own drawings or those copied from a book. Fashion them from soft wood, available at most craft or hobby stores that can be cut with a razor blade.
- Hang those decorated toys together to create a mobile.
- Stencil a simple design on a cupboard door, on the wall adjacent to a corner or over a door, or around a door frame. Keep it light, but colorful.
- Stencil a design on a corner or along the side of a picture frame.
- If you get really hooked on stencils, consider a design that stretches around the wall like a chair rail.
- Most craft stores have stencils of large letters in a variety of styles that can be used to create a motto or saying.

over a doorway, over a fireplace, or along a part of the wall at chair rail height.

• For stenciled decorations, use a water–based paint that can be easily removed before it dries when you make a mistake. Once dry, buff the stencil lightly with very fine sandpaper or steel wool to reduce the intensity of the color and create an antique look.

Check out craft shows on television and your local crafts store for more ideas that you can use.

Paint, dye or stencil a rug. Buy an inexpensive plain wicker rug and hang it from a line out–of–doors. Color it with spray paint or fabric dye applied with a brush. Uneven application is okay—it will give the rug character. Use several colors to create a pattern or free–hand design. Just be sure not to get paint or dye on anything you don't want colored, and allow the rug to dry thoroughly. Paint or dye that isn't dry may cause the rug to stick to the floor, could transfer color to the floor, and might promote the growth of mold.

A rug made up of squares that are tied together can be taken apart and alternate squares dyed different colors to create a checkerboard pattern, then retied.

A stencil pattern can be applied to a rug that is plain, dyed or painted. Paint over the stencils with several coats of a good shellac to prevent wearing off the design.

For a finished look, attach a strip of cloth around the edges of the rug. Make the strip wide enough to create a narrow border around the edges of both the top and bottom of the rug so that either side can be used. Hem the edges of the strip by folding them in about one–quarter of an inch and hot gluing or sewing them.

Dress up a bedroom with a headboard of fabric. Hang a quilt or yard goods by tacking it up at the corners and in the center and let it drape like a swag. Use decorative hangers and attach short strips of ribbon at the corners to give it a finished look.

If you don't want to sew, turn the edges of the fabric in and hot glue them for a smooth edge.

Find an old ornamented trunk and restore it or redecorate it. Placed at the foot of the bed, it can be used to hold extra linens or blankets.

Decorating with Plants

Use plants to bring a touch of the outdoors inside, brighten a room, and create a comfortable, homey look.

Exchange plants between the outdoors and inside. We have several plants that are brought inside for a time, usually four to five weeks. Then they go back out to the sunshine and are replaced by others.

DECORATING

Boston Ferns grow well inside, but they have to be misted frequently. This can be beneficial during dryer seasons when a daily misting will add moisture to the air in the room as well.

Best not to hang them over electronic equipment, such as the television or stereo, or over fine furniture, none of which would appreciate getting wet.

Turn that aquarium into a terrarium or aquatic plant garden. Who needs fish? An attractive, well–lit aquarium used as a home for tropical or aquatic plants can be an interesting focal point for a room and it requires very little care.

A large plant can help to pull a room together, and like tall furniture, a tall plant will make the ceiling seem lower.

Select plants that will thrive indoors and require only the amount of care that you are willing to give them.

Place plants according to the amount of sunlight they need, whether a lot or a little.

When selecting pots for plants, be sure to allow for drainage and adequate room to grow.

HANDY HOUSEHOLD HINTS

Consider an unusual container such as a coffee mug, bowl, or wastebasket. Just remember the rule about drainage.

Protect furniture and carpets by placing pots on trivets that allow air to circulate underneath and prevent moisture from forming.

When reusing an old pot, wash it well and disinfect with a solution of water and chlorine bleach to prevent passing on fungus from the last plant.

Beware of plant overcrowding. To keep plants healthy as they grow bigger, transplant them to larger pots or divide them and transplant in additional pots, whichever best suits your decor.

When leaving plants unattended for a week or more, create a mini–greenhouse by covering them with plastic trash bags to prevent a loss of moisture due to evaporation. Be sure that the soil is damp, but not soggy.

Water house plants with water at room temperature. Most plants don't mind chlorine, but it doesn't hurt to allow tap water to stand for a day to release the chlorine.

When you clean out the fish tank, save the old water for the plants. It contains plenty of nutrients that they love.

The water used for boiling eggs is excellent for watering plants.

To tell if a house plant needs water, stick your finger in the soil to a depth of one inch. If the soil is damp, water is not needed.
If you can't easily insert a finger into the soil, perhaps the plant needs repotting.

Water your plants while you are away by placing them in a couple of inches of water in the bathtub. Towels placed under them will raise them out of the water and act as a siphon to feed an adequate supply of water through the drainage hole in the bottom of the pot.

If you leave plants outdoors, put them in the tub for a thorough watering when they come back in. The water will drive out most insects that may have invaded the soil.

To shine leaves, apply a little glycerin with a soft cloth to the top surface.

Check plants often for dead leaves and remove them. They are unattractive, contribute nothing, and rob the plant of precious nutrients.

Prolong the life of cut flowers by cutting the stems at an angle with a sharp knife, trimming off any leaves that may rot in the water, and adding an aspirin tablet or a mixture of one tablespoon of vinegar and one tablespoon of sugar to each pint of water.

Preserve cut flowers by spraying them lightly with hair spray.

Create a plant sculpture. And it requires very little artistic talent. You will need a flat or wide–mouthed container— size and shape are your choice—and a styrofoam block of the type used for flower arranging. Cut the block to fit in the bottom of the container and cover it with tissue paper or aluminum foil. Gather a variety of dried weeds (you can buy dried flowers, but the weeds work as well), and arrange them by sticking them in the styrofoam block. Once you are satisfied with the arrangement, spray it with metallic gold or silver taking care to lightly cover every surface. Voila! A metallic flower sculpture that can grace a mantle, a dining table or a buffet.
Some suggestions:
• Look for a variety of long reeds and stalks—once you begin to notice them, you will be amazed at the variety you pass every day along the road.

DECORATING

- Don't be concerned about color; remember, you're going to spray them.
- Start the arrangement loosely with stalks scattered over the surface of the block, then balance it out by filling in the empty spaces.
- If you aren't satisfied with your first effort, try again. Every one you do will be different, and you've only expended a few materials and a little time on each.

Feeling Good

It's a State of Mind

Be kinder to yourself
by setting aside time to relax, to meditate, to read,
or just to do something you want to do for yourself.

Give up the pressure of demanding instant gratification.
There is no technique for unwinding that fits everyone—
you need to find the one that fits you and make it a regular part of your life, whether it's daily yoga or bi-weekly
aerobics, an hour daily for knitting or some other hobby
other than cleaning.
How about or a weekly long distance telephone call or a
letter to a friend or relative who is special to you?
Allow time for the new 'habit' to become an established
part of your life to help eliminate old tensions.

If you can't get something out of your mind, it's usually
because you consider it important and are afraid you will
forget it, or are afraid that it will remain unresolved. Keep
a pad around to write down those nagging thoughts so
that you can relax your mind.
If it's a problem that's bothering you, writing down
thoughts as they occur will often help your subconscious
mind lead you to the solution that's been eluding your
conscious mind. It really works!

Making a list of the things you need or want to do is a good way to keep from cluttering your mind. Using the list can be the key to peace of mind—when a task is done, cross it off for a feeling of accomplishment.

Periodically you may want to scan your list and remove any items that are no longer important. We're not in total agreement about this, however—you may find that shortening the list is comforting or you may be distressed by casting off the tasks you couldn't accomplish. Just be sure to do that which makes you most comfortable.

Delegating someone else to take care of a necessary chore and making sure that it gets done may be just as satisfying as doing it yourself.

Or use your list as a journal... When tasks are completed, mark them as such, but don't discard your lists. Over time you will have a running tally of your accomplishments to look back on with pride.

If it's a small task that's nagging you, you may want to just go ahead and do it; then relax knowing you have accomplished something.

Avoid artificial deadlines. Setting goals is great, but don't allow unrealistic goals to take the pleasure out of things you enjoy doing.

We often joke about the notes or materials for little projects that we have stashed away here and there. But we don't allow them to become a burden, nor do we ever give up hope. They are fun projects, not essential ones, and when the right time comes, they will be completed. And it doesn't matter how many are completed; there's always another fun project stored away somewhere.

Prioritizing and planning tasks within a realistic time frame is essential so that you will recognize the times when you simply have to admit that your plate is full—but not always to the same person and not always to your own needs.

When a large task threatens to overwhelm you, break it down into smaller tasks. Take ten minutes each morning to clean a book shelf, polish a piece of furniture, or clean a glass door, for example. Then, when the time comes to clean that room, the period you would normally take can be shortened to fit your busy schedule.

Clean out a closet, a dresser or file cabinet that is making you unhappy with its clutter. Even if you only sort and organize the material you will ease your mind because the project is one step closer to completion.

Cull out and give away or toss out clothing that doesn't fit, and other items that you don't plan to use. You may not want to be reminded of diets that didn't work or unfinished projects that are no longer of interest.

Have a garage sale! It's a great incentive to clean out the closets and other storage spaces, get rid of useless (to you) stuff, and make a little money while doing it.

Throw a party to lift your spirits. Planning for even a small gathering can be a positive reinforcement and give us a reason to wash the windows.

Create a peaceful atmosphere! The family may think you've gone weird on them when you start placing lighted candles around the room, but they can calm the frenetic atmosphere in a room.

Change the pace with a change of clothes. Take a tip from *Mister Rogers* who makes it a point to change his shoes when he comes indoors. Get out of your work clothes and discard that vestige of your workday.

Whether you dress up or down, just the look and feel of fresh clothing can give you a fresh outlook.

BATH

Take time out for a relaxing bath or shower to wash away fatigue or when you feel pressed.

At the end of the work day, it's a great way to shift gears. Sure, you still have a lot to do, but now you are the boss of your time.

Bathe Japanese style. First, take a hot shower to cleanse your skin followed by a cold shower to open the pores.

Then wrap up to keep warm while you run a hot bath; climb in, lie back, and relax.

Use a piece of foam rubber for a back rest in the tub. A thick towel folded over a couple of times can also make a luxurious back rest.

Put lemon slices in the bath water. Hot water leeches out the lemon juice to cleanse your skin and the bathroom will smell great for a long time after.

For a really decadent treat, add a gallon of milk, a pint of honey, and the petals from a rose or other fragrant flower to the hot water in a bathtub and soak in it for twenty minutes.

Sounds terribly wasteful, but where else can you have this much fun for a couple of bucks.

As an added bonus, when you rinse out the tub you may be surprised at how clean it is.

Personal Care Tips—Skin

To clear skin of minor recurring blemishes, use raw egg yolk. Apply freshly separated egg yolk to the skin and allow it to remain for ten to fifteen minutes, then rinse and pat dry. Continue treatment every day for about a month or until condition clears; thereafter, use the treatment about once a week.

For a facial scrub, make a paste of dry oatmeal, water and honey. Rub it on and allow it to remain for ten to fifteen minutes while you relax. Wash off by rubbing gently, using the oatmeal particles as little scouring pads. Follow with a wash of water mixed with a few drops of cider vinegar and allow your face to dry in the air.

Try a facial sauna. Place a large bowl on a towel and fill it with a quart of water heated to boiling; mix with one-quarter cup of Epsom salts, and the juice and shell of half a lemon. Tie back your hair and drape a towel over your head and the bowl; allow the steam to rise up from the bowl and bathe your face. Stay ten to twelve inches above the water at first to avoid steam burn.

For comfort, use a low table or a high stool that will place you well above the level of the bowl. After fifteen minutes, splash on cold water to close pores.

For a skin treat, put cold mineral water in a spray bottle and spray on cleaned skin after steaming or bathing.

A good cleanser for your skin is a solution of one table-spoon of apple cider vinegar to one cup of water. The vinegar not only cleans, but restores the natural acid balance of the skin.

Personal Care Tips—Nails
❋

Protect your fingernails. Before working with grease or paint, scratch a bar of soap to force a protective layer under the nails.

A great nail treatment begins by soaking nails in cooked oatmeal diluted with warm water and the juice of half a lemon. Make it a thin mixture of about one–half cup of water to a heaping spoonful of oatmeal.
Rinse and brush nails gently with a nail brush. Pat dry and push the cuticles upward gently.

Make fingernails shine by rubbing vigorously with the yellow side of a lemon peel, then buffing with a soft cloth.

Use fresh nail polish—it works best. Nail polish is inexpensive, so throw away the old stuff, unless it's a color you simply must have and you can't find it anywhere. Then...

Revive a bottle of nail polish that has thickened by loosening the cap and allowing it to rest in a pan of hot water for a minute or two.

To hold a split nail in place until it grows out, coat the split with clear household cement .

Nail brushing helps keep cuticles healthy. Keep a nail brush in the shower or bath for daily use on both fingers and toes.

Take care of your feet by brushing toe nails every time you bathe or shower to get rid of dead cuticle matter, then dry each toe by rubbing gently with a soft towel and gently pushing back the cuticles.

Personal Care Tips—Hair

Place a non-metal container outside to collect rain water, which is reputed to be a good hair rinse.

Beer is a great tonic and setting gel for your hair. Be sure it is flat (no bubbles) and pour it over your hair after the final rinse, or dip your comb in a glass of beer and moisten your hair as you roll it in curlers. Allow hair to dry thoroughly before unrolling.

A great treatment to make hair shiny: Begin by running very hot water over a couple of towels in the clothes washer, then going through the spin cycle to remove excess water; or wet a towel, wring it out well and microwave it for one to two minutes. Next, apply one-half cup of mayonnaise to dry hair and cover with a plastic shower cap. Make a turban with one of the hot towels and keep it on for twenty minutes, replacing with a fresh hot towel as necessary. Finally, rinse hair with plain water a few times and shampoo thoroughly.

A beneficial hair rinse for dark hair can be made by adding one-quarter cup of dried or fresh rosemary leaves to a pint of boiling water. Steep for about fifteen minutes and strain; use after shampooing.
Extra mixture keeps well in the refrigerator.

Make blonde hair bright with a rinse of a few tablespoons of lemon juice in the water.

Bring out the highlights of red hair with half a cup of vinegar in a quart of water.

Brushing hair with a clean brush between shampoos will remove loose dirt and help redistribute the hair's natural oils.

Clean combs and brushes by soaking in warm water with a couple of tablespoonfuls of baking soda and bleach added.

Personal Care Tips—Eyes

Avoid eye stress by wearing sunglasses. Where there is snow, sand, or water to reflect light, even on cloudy days, sunglasses are as necessary as in the summer sun.

When your eyes are tired, a good pair of polarized sunglasses can be relaxing indoors as well as out.

For tired eyes, lay a thin slice of cucumber over each eye, allowing the cucumber to extend below the eye. Turn slice over to be cool on your skin for five to ten minutes.

To relax the eyes, try a technique called 'palming'. Rest the elbows on a table or desk top; cover the eyes with the hands placed so that the little fingers are in line with the nose and the tips of the fingers are resting on the forehead. Cup the hands so as to shut out all light without putting pressure on the eyeball. Keep the eyes in total darkness for at least three minutes.

This procedure can be an effective means to relax the mind and body as well as the eyes in the midst of a busy day or at the end of one.

For overnight eye care, dab unscented castor oil very gently all around the eye and along 'crow's feet'.

Avoid the lash line to keep the oil out of your eyes.

Old mascara can be revived in a pinch by placing the tube in a glass of hot water for a few minutes.

Generally, however, because of the tendency of bacteria to build up in mascara, we recommend replacement when the tube begins to dry out.

Eye diseases are easily transmitted, so we recommend against the sharing of eye makeup.

Tippled Too Much?

Before going to bed, try:
- a couple of aspirin;
- a teaspoonful of sugar; or
- eating something light that is protein-rich, such as a scrambled egg or a slice of lunch meat.

Alcohol robs the body of minerals, so take a mineral tablet. Be careful of vitamin pills; if they contain a lot of niacin, it may keep you awake with a niacin 'rush'.

For the morning after, try soaking in a warm tub fortified with a cup of Epsom salts to detoxify your body.

An upset stomach can sometimes be settled by weak tea.

Another stomach settler is unbuttered toast or unsalted crackers.

To counteract dehydration, try juice diluted with water at room temperature; be careful of drinking too much water—it can take you back to the earlier condition that got you into this fix in the first place.

A little foresight can help:
- **Don't over–imbibe.** Perhaps easier said than done, but it helps if you begin with a positive attitude and determination not to fall into the trap.
- **Consuming yogurt or other milk products** prior to drinking alcoholic beverages is said to help protect the stomach from distress.
- **Make the next one water.** At a gathering where everyone will regularly have a drink in hand, make at least every second drink water—you'll feel much better in the morning.

Notes on This and That

When a facial or hair treatment requires time to work, you may want to relax and enjoy it or you may find it a good time to read the mail, pay bills or complete some other task that is nagging at you and creating tension in your life.

Brush your hair before you wash it to reduce the loose hairs that can clog up the drain.

Clean hair deserves clean tools. Soak brushes and combs for about five minutes in warm water into which a liberal helping of baking soda has been dissolved. Comb through the brush to loosen and remove hairs and lint—this will clean both brush and comb. Rinse well.

When using hair spray, cover the ears. Even small amounts of the spray can build up inside the ear and prove detrimental over time.

Remember your ears when applying moisturizer and sun block. The skin on the outer edge of the ear is very sensitive and susceptible to damage by the hot rays of the sun.

For a more comfortable and closer shave, rub on a little baby oil before applying shaving cream.

If you tweeze your brows, consider waxing instead. It's fast and inexpensive, and many hair salons offer the service to walk–in clientele.
See how the professionals do it and find out if you like it before investing in home products.

Don't be too aggressive with your plucking! Light tweezing to reshape brows and tidy up scraggly tips is usually sufficient to improve your appearance.

Experiment over a few weeks. If you find plucking too uncomfortable or too tedious, allow the brows to grow back and use a little brush dampened with hair spray to shape brows.

Clear mascara can be brushed on to help tame bushy brows.

To help your perfume or cologne keep its fragrance longer, oil your skin before applying.

Health Tips

𝓣𝓱𝓮 𝓣𝓱𝓲𝓷𝓰𝓼 𝓦𝓮 𝓔𝓪𝓽

❀ ❀ ❀

If you feel you need to lose weight, but aren't ready for a strict diet, try an *almost diet*. Cut down on some of the richer foods and sauces.

❀ ❀ ❀

To reduce calories, cut out one calorie-rich item or use a low calorie substitute in at least one dish for each meal.

❀ ❀ ❀

Eliminate a source of fat such as mayonnaise, butter, or high–fat commercial desserts.
Start slowly—drop one item every week or two. You will soon see the difference if you are diligent.

To reduce the temptation to overeat, avoid creating leftovers. Make just enough for one serving or make enough for two meals and freeze the second one <u>immediately</u> after it is prepared.

❋ ❋ ❋

Consult the food pyramid for recommended portions of fat, veggies, etc. and compare them with your normal intake. Plan meals to include more of the things you need and less of those that are not beneficial so that intake isn't reduced so much as to make you uncomfortable.

❋ ❋ ❋

Become proficient in meal planning and preparation, and eating habits will improve. Proper planning may take some serious thought and research at first, but over time it will become automatic, resulting in better health.

As you start to feel better, then feel really good, you will find that you have more energy and everything you do becomes easier and more gets done.

❋ ❋ ❋

Pay attention to eating habits. If a person hiccups or belches after eating, it's a good bet that he or she is a 'gulp and gobble' eater.

Slow down. Chew each bite well and enjoy.

❋ ❋ ❋

If you are in the habit of eating from a tray while you sit in front of the television, try to make at least one meal a week a dining experience while seated at the dinner table for a delightful change.

Ailments

Get rid of dust for good health as well as for cosmetic appeal. Dust not only looks bad, it contains particles of hair, dead skin, fine sand and dirt, plant spores, pollen, lint, insect parts, chemical residue, and bacteria, any of which can trigger illness and allergies.

Keep the air clean during cold and flu season by changing air filters every three to four weeks. Mark your calendar as a reminder.

When you catch a cold, the best cure seems to be rest. Take careful stock of the things you need to do, prioritize them and eliminate all but the essentials to relieve tension and allow yourself to rest.

❅ ❅ ❅

Take care not to reinfect yourself and others. Germs on the hands are easily transmitted via door knobs, drawer pulls, faucet handles, the telephone, etc. Wash hands with soap and water as often as possible.

We have seen a recommendation by one medical authority who suggests not covering the mouth when coughing or sneezing, but only turning the head aside because of the tendency to spread germs with the hands. We, on the other hand, remain firm in the belief that one who does not cover the mouth and then wash the hands is doomed to perdition.

❋ ❋ ❋

After washing hands, be sure to wash the faucet handles and the bar of hand soap that can become a breeding ground for germs.
Liquid soap is becoming increasingly popular. It keeps germs out of the soap, but you still need to rinse the container after each use.

❋ ❋ ❋

Keep a spray bottle of alcohol handy and use it. Periodically, pass through the house to spray and wipe any of the areas we regularly touch with our hands.
Be sure to clearly mark the bottle as 'ALCOHOL'.

❋ ❋ ❋

To help sleep, try a Hot Toddy. Mix together the juice from half a lemon, a teaspoon of honey, six ounces of hot water and a dollop of whiskey. Drink it down and hop into bed.

❋ ❋ ❋

Another old home remedy to help sweat out a cold—wash the outside of one or two grapefruit thoroughly and cut the skin and fruit into chunks. (Of course if you want to eat some of the fruit, it couldn't hurt.)
Cover the chunks with an inch or so of water in a saucepan and simmer for about an hour. Mash and stir from time to time, adding more water if necessary to maintain the water level in the pan.
Strain off the juice, sweeten with honey if desired, and drink at least a cup of the mixture while it is still warm. Go to bed and bundle up well. The hot liquid and the

quinine extracted from the rind will make you perspire freely, so avoid any drafts.

This is best administered in the evening or at a time when you can expect to sleep at least two or three hours. It only tastes bad, it doesn't make you feel bad. Its purpose is to help the body naturally 'sweat out' the illness, in the same manner as the toddy.

We call the grapefruit concoction described above, 'tonic'. It freezes well, so we keep a stack of ziplock bags full during the cold and flu season.

There may be a side benefit as well. The kids don't like the stuff, but they know it's there, so they think twice about faking illness to stay home from school.

Take an Epsom salts bath. Dissolve a couple of cups of Epsom salts in a warm bath water and soak for no longer than twenty minutes. Then shower and dry well.

This is especially effective when you first feel a cold coming on.

To relieve a sore throat, gargle with a mixture of half a teaspoon of salt in three ounces of warm water. It tastes nasty, but it usually works.

Tissues are still a basic weapon against colds! Germs from a sneeze can drift through a house for hours, especially if the air is warm and moist from bathing or cooking.

Place boxes of tissues in strategic locations throughout the house along with a plastic bag for disposing of used tissues. Don't empty the bags; just close them tightly and throw them out; replace them frequently.

❋   ❋   ❋

Flush dirty tissues down the toilet whenever practical to avoid germ pools in the waste basket.

❋   ❋   ❋

Sanitize waste baskets with a mixture of alcohol and water sprayed inside and out.

❋   ❋   ❋

Make a disinfectant from a cup of water, a couple of drops of liquid dish detergent and two ounces (four tablespoons) of rubbing alcohol. Use in the bathroom, kitchen and sickroom.
Keep tightly capped between uses and add more alcohol if necessary to compensate for evaporation.

❋   ❋   ❋

To sanitize bedding, remove it from the bed carefully, folding in toward the center in order to capture bacteria, etc., then wash in hot water with detergent.

❋   ❋   ❋

Treat poison ivy with a paste of uncooked oatmeal and water. Dab the paste on the infected area, and allow it to dry and remain.

❋   ❋   ❋

A thorough washing with yellow bar soap as soon as possible after contact with poison ivy will often prevent an outbreak.

❋   ❋   ❋

HEALTH TIPS

Keep an aloe plant for medicinal purposes. The liquid in the center of the leaf is excellent for treating burns, sunburn, and most skin irritations including chapped lips and irritation from blowing the nose.

Pinch off the tip of a leaf and squeeze out the liquid, or slice off an entire leaf, use what you need, and freeze the leaf. It only takes a few moments to thaw the next time you need it.

Car Care

Cleaning

Use only clean rags to wash and dry the car. The tiniest bit of abrasive material in a rag can do terrible things to the finish.

In the same vein, resist the temptation to rest packages on the car while you open a door or the trunk—bits of dust, pollen, and the like will eventually be ground into the finish and scratch it.

Get rid of tar spots on the car by covering them with raw linseed oil and allowing the oil to remain until the spots are soft, then wiping them up with a soft cloth containing some of the oil.

Peanut butter will remove tar! Cover spots of tar with peanut butter, allow it to remain for about an hour, and wipe it off.

CAR CARE

Remove rust spots from chrome with very fine (0000) steel wool. Coat the chrome with a good quality car wax to prevent, or at least retard, reappearance of the rust.

To get rid of rust on the chrome, scrub it with a wad of aluminum foil, then coat with gray or clear wax crayon to protect the metal.

Toss floor mats in the dryer periodically to shake out the dirt. Allow them to tumble without heat. Be sure to clean out the lint trap afterward.

When you change wiper blades, save the best of the used ones to squeegee side windows or condensation on the inside of the windows.

When you wash windows, don't forget the inside. Dust and cigarette smoke leave a film of grease that promotes fogging. Polish the glass to a clear shine.

Eliminate cigarette odor in the car with a layer of dry baking soda in the bottom of the ash tray. It will extinguish smoldering cigarettes and freshen the air.
Get in the habit of emptying the ashtrays regularly to keep the vehicle smelling fresh.

Keep an old toothbrush with the auto cleaning supplies. It's great for getting into small spaces when you clean the inside of the car.

To get rid of fresh oil spots in the carport, cover with kitty litter and sweep up after the oil is absorbed.

Corn starch will soak up oil spots. Sprinkle corn starch over the area and sweep up after the oil is absorbed.

For old oil spots, soften with mineral spirits, then pick up with kitty litter or cornstarch as described above. Repeat if necessary.

Stubborn old oil spots can be lifted by first dampening the spot with warm water and bleach; one part bleach to four parts water. Cover the stain with powdered laundry detergent and allow to remain for about an hour. Remoisten area as necessary to maintain a damp paste.
Allow to dry, then brush the area and rinse well. Repeat if necessary.

Maintenance

Don't wait for a trouble light to tell you something is wrong. Take a few minutes on a regular basis, once every week or two, for a simple maintenance check:

- Check the oil, steering, and transmission fluids.
- Make sure there is coolant in the reserve tank.
- Look over the hoses for any that are dry or cracking. Hoses are inexpensive; stalling out in a remote area for want of a heater or vacuum hose is not.
- Check air pressure in the tires. Improper inflation will shorten the life of a tire.
- Visually inspect tires for uneven wear—an inside or outside tread that is worn down more than the rest of the tread calls for a trip to the garage. Misalignment will shorten the life of the tire and pose an unsafe driving condition.

Keep a list of things to be checked regularly so that none will be overlooked.

If you have difficulty seeing the *add* and *full* lines on the oil dip stick, drill tiny holes at the lines or scribe with a file to make them easier to read.

When pouring from a rectangular oil or gas can with an opening near one end, pour with the spout end up for a nice even flow. When the opening is below the level of the liquid in the can, air cannot enter to replace that being poured out, causing the liquid to come out in spurts.

Check the battery terminals each time you check the oil. White powdery residue is a sign of corrosion and can indicate a loose connection that can overwork you battery and ultimately cause it to fail.

Clean battery terminals with a wire brush and make sure the connection is tight. The most common cause of a failed battery is a loose or corroded connection.
And don't forget to check the ground wire connection.

After cleaning terminals, coat them with petroleum jelly to keep corrosion from reforming.

If you don't have a sealed battery, check the water level and add distilled water as necessary.

An older battery, over two years, should be checked periodically at a garage equipped to do so. They can determine that the battery is maintaining a full charge. This is especially important in cold weather areas before the onset of winter.

CAR CARE

Check the windshield wipers when you check the oil. A windshield wiper that is worn may be revived by rubbing lightly with fine sandpaper, but they are so inexpensive and easy to replace that it is hardly worth the effort except in an emergency.

If you change your own oil, remember to change the filter as well.

Used oil should be taken to a recycling center—check with your local environmental protection agency for a drop off location.

Cover the oil filter with a plastic bag before removing it to catch all the goo.

Store funnels and tools in a plastic bag to keep them from attracting dust.

Keep leftover lubricants clean with the plastic top from a food can, or cover the top with a plastic bag.

Check tire pressure regularly to prevent excessive strain and uneven wear on the tires, to save gas, and to insure safe operation of the vehicle.

HANDY HOUSEHOLD HINTS

The best way to insure even tire wear and longer life is proper alignment. Exchanging front and back tires every six months or six thousand miles also helps.

It's time for new tires when a penny inserted into the shallowest tread doesn't go past the top of Lincoln's head.

Replacing burned out bulbs is not difficult—most are reached from under the hood or inside the trunk. Check your local auto supply store for the correct bulb; they may even be willing to help you replace it.

Replacing headlights is a little more complicated; they need to be checked by a mechanic to be sure they are aimed properly.

After replacing headlights and having them adjusted, mark on your garage wall exactly where the point of the beam hits. Then if they get out of adjustment you will spot it quickly.

Turn the air conditioning on occasionally in the winter and the heat on in the summer to keep them working properly and prevent fungus from forming.

Troubleshooting

Keep an emergency kit in the car: In addition to your spare tire and jack, include:
- a flashlight, preferably one that has a blinker attached
- jumper cables
- flares
- duct tape
- spare fuses
- an empty gas can with a spout
- a can of oil
- a tire inflation kit
- waterless cleaner and paper towels, or moist wipes for cleaning hands after roadside repairs
- an adjustable wrench, a couple of screwdrivers, and a small knife.

You may want more tools depending on your knowledge and skill.

When your car lock freezes, heat the key. Hold it with a glove or handkerchief to avoid burning your hands. Don't force the key. The heat should gradually free the frozen tumblers, but if it doesn't, you don't need a broken key to add to your troubles.

When you get stuck on ice or snow, place rubber floor mats under the tires to gain traction.

If you don't have an ice scraper, in an emergency use a credit card.

When you run out of gas and don't have a funnel, use a manila envelope with a corner cut to the size opening you need to pour gas from a can into your tank.

A temporarily patch for a leaky hose can be made using chewing gum, then tying a rag around the hose to hold the gum in place.

Use duct tape for temporary repairs to a broken hose.

If you are caught out on the road with a bad windshield wiper blade, try exchanging it with the one on the passenger side for a temporary fix. If the blade has been broken off, tape something over the bare metal end of the arm to keep it from scratching the windshield.

When the wipers fail, a cola drink may help! Pouring the soda over the windshield causes the rain to sheet off—doesn't last long, but it may help you get to a shop where you can buy a replacement blade.

When filling up at a self–service station, place the gas cap on the steering column or the front seat to avoid driving off without it.

CAR CARE

When shopping at the mall, tie a ribbon to the top of the car antennae to make it easier to locate your car later.

Keep a couple of those plastic grocery bags in the car— they make dandy trash bags.

To keep jumper cables from tangling, stretch them full length and tape them together in several places.

In wintry weather, keep a couple of plastic jugs full of sand in the trunk. If you get stuck, you can pour the sand on ice to gain traction.

Keep a thick towel in the car to drape over the steering wheel when you park on a hot day. It will keep the wheel cooler and can be placed on the seat to keep you cool when you drive.

Traveling

Plan your trip—write or call for maps and information about the areas you plan to visit. Get the phone number or address of the state Tourism Bureau or Chamber of Commerce from their respective offices in your area.

Place a call to directory assistance in the city you plan to visit for the number of a local tourist or convention bureau. They will not only have information about local attractions and the best times to visit, but should be able to recommend hotels and eateries as well.

Check out the State Welcome Stations along the way. They usually offer maps and a rack full of materials about local or regional attractions. We have found them to be a great source of information about those that are newest or lesser known.

Why take a chance with hotels or motels? Most have an 800 number that you can call for reservations.
But if it's off season and you want to haggle over rates, call the motel of your choice at their local number and ask to speak to a manager.

If you want a better rate, but don't feel up to bargaining, contact a travel agent. He or she may have access to very nice rooms at special rates, especially in the off season.

When you make a reservation, remember to state your preferences, such as a non–smoking room, one on a lower or upper floor, connecting rooms, etc.

When you arrive, ask to see the room before checking in, especially in an older establishment.

Before you leave, arrange with someone to pick up the paper and the mail.

If the trip is for an extended period you may want to suspend delivery of the paper and ask the post office to hold your mail. Check with the post office well ahead of the planned trip to find out how much advance notice they require.

Put lamps on timers so that your house doesn't appear unoccupied at night.

Ask a friend to stop by to occasionally check the house. A leaking water pipe or heater can be a disaster if left to run for a week.

If more than one person is checking on the house, make sure they know about each other to prevent a false alarm.

Perhaps you have a neighbor who is willing to park a car in your driveway to make the house appear occupied.

Make a checklist, of things to do before you go and items to take. It's easy to forget details in the last minute confusion of packing and leaving.

It's a terrible thing to be miles from home when you realize the you have forgotten something.

Take a map, even if you have directions for getting to your destination—there's no way to anticipate a detour because of road construction. ...And you may spot an attraction worthy of a detour.

On long auto trips, take along a pillow covered with several pillowcases. As the pillowcases get dirty, remove them one at a time and use the soiled ones to hold dirty laundry.

Take along a night light—use it in your motel room so that if you wake up in the night you can quickly orient yourself to the unfamiliar surroundings.

Containers in your toilet kit such as shampoo can be placed in zip lock bags to contain any spills.

When packing for a long trip, take a small bag with only the toilet articles, clothes, etc. needed for a couple of days. That way, you don't have to unpack everything every time you stop.

To remove wrinkles from a garment when unpacking, hang it in the bathroom and run the shower on very hot for a couple of minutes.

Carry prescription drugs in their original containers when traveling far from home. It will make life a lot easier if you need a refill. ...And may prevent the need for embarrassing explanations if you are stopped by the police.

Pack small items in shoes to save space and make them easier to find when you want them.

Use an old pair of socks to cover shoes and protect clean clothing.

Stash an extra set of keys in the trunk. If you lose your keys or lock them in the car, the trunk is easiest to break into. If you keep an extra trunk key in your wallet or purse, you won't have to break in.

If you like to snack on trips, make a permanent care package—a small travel bag containing a can opener, eating utensils and canned goods, as well as a list of items to add at the last minute, such as cheese and crackers. For wakeup coffee or tea include an immersion heater, cups, instant coffee, cream, etc.

Keep ice in plastic ziplock bags in the cooler—it eliminates having to wipe everything down as you remove it and ensures that the ice will be clean if you want to use it in drinks.

You can also freeze a plastic container of water or fruit juice. As it defrosts, it will keep other items cool.

For a trip to the beach, lay down pile carpet scraps throughout the car—even on the seats. The carpet will catch and hold most of the sand clinging to clothes when you leave. A little talcum powder dusted on the feet will make it easier to remove sand that clings to your skin before you get in the car.

Odds & Ends

To save gas and improve mileage around town, cut down on weight! Fill the gas tank only half way and get rid of unnecessary items in the trunk or back of a truck.

To improve mileage, remove devices that create drag such as bike and ski racks that are not being used.

Driving at speeds of 45 to 55 miles per hour gets the best mileage for most vehicles.

Fast acceleration wastes gas and tires.

Protect fragile items you are transporting by buckling them in with a seat belt.

CAR CARE

When carrying more small items than will fit in the trunk, place a box on the seat and strap it in with a seat belt. Small items can be better protected in the box and if you stop short they won't go flying around inside the car.

In the event that your car dies, turn on the flashers immediately and get the car off the road as quickly as possible. Raise the hood to alert others if you don't have a cellular phone to call for help or the State Police.

Take a moment to find the switch for your flashers and turn them on and off a few times so that the movement will be automatic in an emergency.

Extra sets of keys stashed on your person or under the vehicle, and in a safe place at home can be a life saver if you lose the ones you are carrying. When you pull out that emergency set, head for the locksmith to get another.

Garage Sales

Planning

Do a quick survey of the things you have to sell. Make sure its enough to be worth the trouble. It will also give you some idea of the amount of time you need to prepare them and the space you need to display them such as tables, racks for clothing, etc.

Pick a date far enough in advance to allow time to gather the sale items, clean them if necessary and price them.

A good way to learn about garage sales and to get ideas is to attend a couple of sales in your neighborhood.

Check with your local newspaper for information. Many newspaper offices furnish garage sale kits that include signs, suggestions for advertising, and tips for running a successful garage sale.

GARAGE SALES

Write the classified ad. Be sure to include the address, dates and hours, an alternate date in case of rain, and whether or not early birders are welcome.

Don't include your phone number in the ad: you don't want to be constantly answering questions over the phone. People can't buy unless they are there!

Joint sales with friends can be fun and will give you more to sell; but your friends should be there to help with advance preparations and on the day of the sale.
Make sure that your friends are there to have fun and get rid of stuff, not for pure greed.

Use different colored tags for each person's belongings. Put the tags in the cash box when you make a sale and add them up when you're ready to split the cash.
Take care to mark the tag if an item was sold for less than the amount shown.

When setting days and hours consider the climate of your neighborhood: some areas aren't inclined to have sales on Sunday, some are. Preferred hours may vary as well.

Locations off the beaten path generally have steady Saturday business only until two or three in the afternoon because garage salers have to go out of their way to see what is available.

Locations along a thoroughfare or a well trafficked street usually have steady business, even if they start Friday afternoon.

Advise close neighbors of your plans so as to avoid objections to the traffic and parking problems. You may even pick up some help or additional merchandise.

Preparation

Enter into the project with the proper attitude:
- Keep in mind that this is not primarily an ongoing, money–making proposition; it's an opportunity to inventory your discardables, get rid of them, and make a bit of extra cash in the process.
- Don't expect people to take care of your items; they are out for a casual day's lark, and sometimes things get broken.
- Don't expect them to be particularly respectful of your possessions, either. You are also on a lark, and shouldn't be disheartened by strangers who cast a disparaging eye on them.

Cleaning and preparing items for sale can be time consuming, so start early, set aside a couple of hours a day and work at it regularly to keep the task from being overwhelming.

GARAGE SALES

Some items just won't sell if they aren't cleaned first, like that barbecue grill full of ashes and drippings.

✳

Items that look like junk won't sell and they'll turn off people to other things you have for sale.

✳

A few minutes with a soft brush on the air vents of a radio, television, typewriter, etc. to remove dust will make them more appealing to prospective buyers.
Try blowing out dust with your hair dryer or sucking it up with a brush attachment on the vacuum cleaner.

✳

A toaster or broiler oven should have crumbs and grease removed; a spritz with a window cleaning product and a soft cloth can make a chrome item look $5 to $10 better.

✳

When selling a tape player, offer a demo, but use a tape that isn't your favorite in case it walks off.

✳

As you start to price items, decide whether you are having the sale to eliminate stuff, make money or both. Leave room for dickering.

✳

The value of an item is based on how you feel about it, not necessarily the original cost or its present retail.

✳

Price mark items so as not to damage them. Ink that can't be washed off plastic or stickers on paper products sitting in the sun won't do.

213

HANDY HOUSEHOLD HINTS

Use string tags, available at office supply stores; tie or pin them on in a conspicuous place.

Tags that can be attached to the item with a piece of string are a bit more trouble, but they look lots better than stick on labels or marking on an item. Don't deface your possessions with permanent markers

Put together groups of like items that are all priced the same and place them on separate tables; make a sign instead of labeling each item. Just watch for items that get moved around and put them back in their proper group.

If items don't all belong to the same seller, keep a list of them when they are sold.

Price clothing to sell— 10¢, 50¢, $1.00. Designer clothes worth much more are best left at a consignment shop.

Separate the good stuff from the "needs mending," "has a bleach spot," "small hole in the knee" stuff and clearly mark each group.

If you have lots of blouses, shorts, socks, etc. you want to get rid of, set them up in a separate spot marked "3 for $1," "5 for $1," etc.

Power tools bring a good price; check ads in the local paper or shopper's guide to see what they are worth. Washers, dryers, air conditioners, and televisions are sometimes better sold through classified ads or a community shopper.

Make signs for the sale as clear as possible, specifying days, dates, and times.

*

Check your city's sign ordinance before posting signs for your sale. If you are near a business district or a major thoroughfare, there may be restrictions on posting signs.

*

It's best to have a helper who can relieve you now and then. If it's not a joint sale, perhaps you can enlist the help of a family member or neighbor for a couple of hours in the middle of the day.

*

Don't leave your things unattended. If you don't have an assistant or a portable phone and feel you just *have* to answer the telephone when it rings, buy an extension that you can sell for a few dollars at the end of the sale.

Setting Up

Place large interesting items in clear view on the lawn or in the driveway.

*

If you don't want garage salers to trample plants or cut through the neighbor's yard, put up "Keep Off" signs and rope off the area.

215

HANDY HOUSEHOLD HINTS

Clearly mark items that are not for sale. Garage salers are a rabid bunch and will try to buy anything. Drape an old sheet or bedspread over items in the area, such as garden hoses or lawn ornaments, that are not for sale.

If there are sale items inside a garage or carport, rope off and mark those items that are not for sale or block off part of the area in some way.

For shelf space, set up two ladders with planks between the rungs. Also makes a good barrier in front of things that are not for sale.

If you are selling the tables, sheets, blankets, etc. on which sale items are placed, make arrangements for pickup after the sale.

Clothes sell better if:
 • they are hung up and easy to see,
 • like items are kept together,
 • they smell clean and fresh.

If you don't have enough table or hanger space for clothing or other items, spread a blanket, plastic drop cloth, table cloth, carpeting or old sheet on the lawn. Expect that the drop cloth will be stepped on; mark it for sale or not as you choose.

Set up an extension cord to test electrical items. Helps to have a bulb and batteries, too.

✳

Set up your check-out station in a strategic location where you can see everyone and be easily seen.

✳

Tapes, records and books should be kept indoors or in a shaded area near your check-out station.

✳

Parents in a shopping frenzy don't always watch the kids too well, so keep valuable or breakable items near the check-out.

✳

Get as much change and singles from the bank as you can afford so that you can break tens and twenties.

✳

You don't have to bother with checks—most garage sales are cash only.

✳

A freebie basket or 2 for 5¢ basket is always fun for getting rid of miscellaneous small items.

✳

Providing bags is a nice touch. Begin saving those from the grocery store as soon as you start planning your sale. Distribute them on an "as needed" basis.

✳

Most garage salers are decent people who comply with your requests and are out to have a good time, so make a bunch of signs like:

Buy Everything!

or

Hi! Hi! Hi!
Buy! Buy! Buy!

A good sense of humor can go a long way!

Day of the Sale

It's a good idea to put signs up on the morning of the sale and take them down as soon as the sale is concluded.

Make a paper trail of signs:
- at the main turns onto your street from each direction;
- if you are near a busy street, post a sign before the approach nearest you and at each corner or turn leading to the sale.

Do a drive–by to make sure that signs are visible and allow drivers enough time to turn or stop before they pass you by.

Always greet shoppers—it sets a pleasant tone, identifies you as the person in charge, and encourages people to stay and browse longer.

✳

People are looking for bargains so be prepared to do some friendly dickering.

✳

Stay with your stuff. Be available to answer questions.

✳

Don't expect those neat piles of clothes to stay that way. Buyers will check and recheck for stains and tears. Straighten them up when you get a chance.

✳

If you use a cash box, stay with it. If you get up to leave, the cash box might do the same.
Don't wander off looking for other items in the midst of the sale with people standing around unless you have an assistant.

✳

An apron with pockets is secure and handy for carrying change and bills.

✳

Separate large bills from the smaller bills you are using to make change. An expensive mistake when making change can take a lot of fun out of the day.

✳

Don't be shy about asking for correct change before your customer pulls out a big bill to pay for a 50¢ purchase.

✳

To conserve change if you run low, round down to a whole dollar. Just say "If you don't have correct change, I'll drop the odd 15¢."

You may get the change, you may get a quarter and be told to keep the change, or your customer may leave feeling he or she got a good deal. Either way, good for you! Garage sales are perfect for small scale wheeling and dealing.

*

You can also conserve change by offering a small item in place of 10¢ or 25¢ in change.

*

Remove the signs in the street before you take in your items unless you want to be pestered by last minute shoppers as you are packing up.